# I HATE

# WORD
## FOR WINDOWS®

### Bryan Pfaffenberger

Shoe ® & ©, 1993, Tribune Media Services, Inc. All Rights Reserved.

I Hate Word for Windows

## Copyright © 1993 by Que ® Corporation

Library of Congress Catalog Card Number: 93-84297

ISBN: 1-56529-256-1

95 94 93      6 5 4 3 2 1

Interpretation of the printing code: the rightmost double-digit number is the year of the book's printing; the rightmost single-digit number, the number of the book's printing. For example, a printing code of 93-1 shows that the first printing of the book occurred in 1993.

Screen reproductions in this book were created using Collage Plus from Inner Media, Inc., Hollis, NH.

*I Hate Word for Windows* is based on Word for Windows Version 2.0.

Cover illustration by Jeff MacNelly.

---

*Publisher:* David P. Ewing

*Associate Publisher:* Rick Ranucci

*Operations Manager:* Sheila Cunningham

*Publishing Plan Manager:* Thomas H. Bennett

*Marketing Manager:* Ray Robinson

# Dedication

To Michael

# Credits

**Title Manager:**
Shelley O'Hara

**Production Editor:**
Lori Cates

**Technical Editor:**
Tish Nye

**Book Designers:**
Scott Cook
Amy Peppler-Adams

**Novice Reviewer:**
Deborah Abshier

**Editorial Assistant:**
Julia Blount

**Production Team:**

| | |
|---|---|
| Jeff Baker | Bob LaRoche |
| Claudia Bell | Jay Lesandrini |
| Danielle Bird | Angela Pozdol |
| Julie Brown | Caroline Roop |
| Brad Chinn | Linda Seifert |
| Lisa Daugherty | Sandra Shay |
| Brook Farling | Tina Trettin |
| Heather Kaufman | Johnna VanHoose |
| Linda Koopman | Alyssa Yesh |

Composed in Goudy and MCPdigital by Que Corporation.

# About the Author

**Bryan Pfaffenberger**, called "Hamburger," "Cheeseburger," and other injurious things during his painful years at school, at last found obscurity as a sincere, mild-mannered, and bumbling professor at a small Midwestern liberal arts college. But this peaceful existence was rudely interrupted after his 1981 purchase of a Kaypro computer, which occasioned a new round of ridicule. After spending a few months learning how to format a disk, Bryan declared to his astonished friends, family, and colleagues, "If I can figure this out, anyone can."

Since then, Bryan has written more than 35 books that translate computer mumbo-jumbo into plain English. An example: his best-selling *Que's Computer User's Dictionary*, with more than 250,000 copies in print.

Bryan knows that computers can help people work better, smarter, and faster, but they can be a pain in the you-know-what. Worse, most computer books throw all the facts at you, as if you had to know *everything*. Isn't that sick?

Que's *I Hate...* books reflect Bryan's philosophy: "Computer books should teach only what you need to know. They should tell you what parts of the program are pointless and forgettable. And they shouldn't ask you to plow through 200 pages of tutorials just so that you can learn how to print a document."

Bryan's writing style gets right to the point, with an informal and humorous approach. With *I Hate Word for Windows* as your guide, you may not end up loving Word for Windows—but you'll know how to fake it.

## Acknowledgments

A lot of people contributed to this book in so many ways.

To Neil Young, thanks for Harvest Moon, which kept me company during long hours at the keyboard.

My editor, Shelley O'Hara, just happens to be the best in the business, and contributed to this book in zillions of ways—thanks, Shelley.

To Rick Ranucci go my thanks for inspiration, guidance, and encouragement. I'd also like to thank my agent, Bill Gladstone, for handling the business stuff so that I could sit around and think up Top Ten lists unperturbed by things like the movie rights to this book (any action there yet, Bill?).

Thanks are due, too, to Que's fantastic editorial team, including Lori Cates, for the usual top-notch job, to Scott Cook for the design, to Jeff MacNelly for the cool cartoons, and to everyone at Que who has worked so hard to bring this book to fruition.

Most of all, thanks to my family for putting up with prolonged bouts at the keyboard.

# Trademark Acknowledgments

All terms mentioned in this book that are known to be trademarks or service marks have been appropriately capitalized. Que cannot attest to the accuracy of this information. Use of a term in this book should not be regarded as affecting the validity of any trademark or service mark.

Microsoft Windows and Microsoft Word for Windows are registered trademarks of Microsoft Corporation.

# Contents at a Glance

# Table of Contents

# Introduction

**"I can't find my document!"**

**"What are these horrible ¶ things?"**

**"Why aren't there page numbers on this printout?"**

**"I *hate* Word for Windows!"**

Sound familiar? If you hate Word for Windows, but you have to use this program at home or at work, you've come to the right place. This book begins with a simple, dangerous, and irreverent premise: Word for Windows isn't worth learning if you have to spend days or weeks being dragged through painful, boring tutorials. If there's something you need to know, you can just look it up.

This book provides an easy, fun introduction to Microsoft Word for Windows. It doesn't try to turn you into a computer-loving vegetable. It includes just enough information about Word to help you get going, produce good work, and get on with the rest of your life.

This is a book I've always wanted to write. I use Word to write all my books—I've used it for years, in all its incarnations (including the DOS and Mac versions). I know exactly which parts of the program are really useful, and which parts are fluff. I'm really excited about sharing this with you because I know it's going to save you a lot of trouble.

## Some Assumptions about You

Let's be frank. You're reading this because you're thinking, "I've got to get some Word skills." But inside you're thinking, "Is there any way I can get out of this?"

If so, welcome to a club recently joined by millions. Like it or not, you have Word, or you've been stuck with this program at work. You've already noticed that the Word manual has more than 800 pages and there are lots of 1200-page books about Word at the bookstore.

So here's the problem. You have more important things to do than spend the next six months taking Word lessons. You're definitely not in love with Microsoft Word. You don't want to have to "learn" stuff, chapter-by-chapter, in a process that goes on for weeks. You don't want to have to memorize anything.

If this picture describes you, congratulations—you're normal, and you have a great chance of succeeding with the computer. I mean that seriously. The people who use computers successfully aren't in love with them; they don't spend time fussing over every little thing for hours and

hours. They just do their work, efficiently and competently, and then shut the darned thing down. You don't have to learn all that stuff!

Are you missing out on anything by following this "only what I need to know" strategy? Nope. I can promise you this: Even if you learn just the stuff in Part I of this book, you'll know enough about Word to use the program intelligently and productively. You can add more skills if you need to. Otherwise, forget about all that intermediate and advanced Word stuff and do something fun.

# About This Book's Icons

**TIP**

This icon alerts you to shortcuts, tricks, or time-savers.

**EXPERTS ONLY**

This icon flags skippable technical stuff that I couldn't resist including. I am, after all, a nerd (although I now understand, after a painful process of self-examination, that most of the rest of the world does not share my enthusiasm for technology).

**CAUTION**

This icon warns you about the pitfalls and traps that make working with Word a little exciting sometimes.

**BUZZWORDS**

This icon alerts you that you're about to be confronted with one of those horrible, heavy-duty computer terms, such as *format* or *macro*.

# And They're Off and Running...

From here, figure out what you need to know. If you can't tell a paragraph mark from a parakeet, start with Chapter 1. If you've already learned how to write, edit, and print with Word, you can begin with Part II or Part III. But remember, this isn't a book to be studied; it's meant to be used, preferably only when you need it. When a question arises, find the answer here—you'll soon be back to work.

# PART I

# Things You Need to Know

**Includes:**

# CHAPTER 1

# Basic Stuff
## (That No One Ever Really Explains)

## IN A NUTSHELL

▼ Turn on the computer and start Windows
▼ Launch Word
▼ Maneuver the mouse
▼ Use menus
▼ Save text
▼ Quit Word

In this chapter, you learn the basics about Word for Windows—the very basics. This chapter contains stuff so simple that you might be embarrassed to ask. But you'll find it here, and no one will know you are reading this. I won't tell.

# Turning on the Computer and Starting Windows

There sits the computer. It's cold. That's because it's off. Let's inject a little juice into this thing and get going.

**TIP**

Your computer won't start correctly if there's a disk in the drive called Drive A, which is usually the top one if you have two drives. If Drive A has a latch thingie that covers the door, you can remove the disk by flipping the latch up so that the disk pops out. If Drive A has no latch but it does have a little button, just push the button, which causes the disk to pop out. There's probably no disk in the drive, but it's better to check before turning on the system. (If you forget, you won't hurt anything, but you'll have to remove the disk and press a key to start over.)

## Where's the Switch?

If you're lucky, your system is hooked up to a *power strip*—an electrical strip with several outlets. (You have to buy the power strip; it doesn't come with the computer.) If so, it's pretty easy to turn on the system: Just flip the switch on the power strip.

If there's no power switch, you have to hunt down the switches for each component. Start with the computer (the box thing) and the monitor (the TV thing).

Look for a button on the front of the computer. Failing that, see if there is a big red switch on the right side of the computer. Be forewarned: Some system designers put the switch on the back panel, where you fear you'll be electrocuted if you stick your finger in the wrong hole, or you may jar loose some of the data cables, resulting in (even more) bizarre system behavior.

As you tenderly but blindly explore the back panel looking for the switch, be careful to avoid the cables, power cords, and large, poisonous bugs and snakes that creep back there seeking warmth and darkness. Monitor switches are even harder to find. Look on the front, back, right side, left side, bottom, and top of the monitor. After that, kick it.

If you found both switches, you'll know it. The computer hums, buzzes, clicks, and whirs. These are happy noises. A great deal of information also flashes past on the screen, much faster than you can read it. You can safely ignore this stuff.

Depending on how your system is set up, Windows might start automatically. You see the Program Manager. If you see a black screen and `C:\>` or `C>`, you're at the DOS prompt (the equivalent of computer hell). Type `WIN` and press the Enter key to start Windows.

# Launching Word (5, 4, 3, 2, 1...Lift-Off!)

If all goes well, you see Program Manager. Program Manager is Windows' launching pad for applications. You launch (start) programs there. When you exit a program, you go back there. Here you see the Word for Windows *program group* window. This is a box-like thing that contains the *icons* (pictures) that you use to start Word.

I HATE WORD FOR WINDOWS!

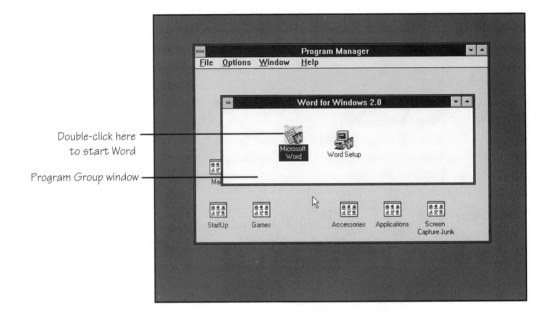

Double-click here to start Word

Program Group window

"I HATE THIS!"

## My Program Manager looks different!

When you exit Windows, the program saves whatever was on Program Manager's screen. If you don't see the Word for Windows thing (window), look at the bottom of the window for an icon (picture) labeled *Word for Windows 2.0*. Move the mouse pointer to the Word for Windows icon and double-click the left mouse button. (To "double-click" means to click the mouse button twice in rapid succession: click-click.)

When you see the Word for Windows icon, you can launch Word. To do so, just move the mouse pointer to the Microsoft Word icon and click the left mouse button twice in rapid succession (this is called *double-clicking*). If it doesn't work the first time, try again. This time, make the clicks closer together.

## What's All This Stuff?

When Word starts, you see the Word screen. There's a lot of junk on this screen, but don't let it overwhelm you. The stuff on-screen makes it easy to access commands. (Your other option is to have your mind cluttered with all the mindless command sequences and key combinations you'd use instead of using the on-screen controls.) You'll come to know the basic pieces gradually, and you can just forget about some of them. Here are the important parts:

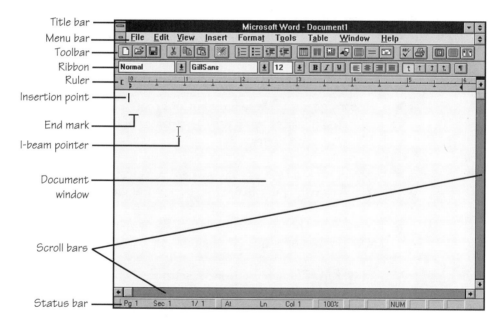

Title bar
Menu bar
Toolbar
Ribbon
Ruler
Insertion point
End mark
I-beam pointer
Document window
Scroll bars
Status bar

**BUZZWORDS**

**DOCUMENT**

A document is any piece of writing that you're working on, such as a poem, letter, report, or the opening volume of a new history of the Roman Empire.

11

**Things you see on your screen**

▼ *Title bar*. This shows the name of the application (Word, obviously). More important, it shows the name of the current *document*. Word starts with a new, untitled document called *Document1*.

▼ *Menu bar*. This shows the names of Word's *menus*. If you click the menu name, a menu pops down. You choose commands from these menus. (If you try this, just click the menu name again to pop the menu back up.)

▼ *Toolbar*. The Toolbar contains buttons you can click to do specific things, such as save your document or print. You learn more about these buttons later in the book, as they become relevant.

▼ *Ribbon and ruler*. These have buttons that help you *format* your text. You'll learn how to use these things in Part III, "Making It Look Nice and Pretty."

▼ *Application workspace*. Here's where you create that timeless prose. You start typing in the next section of this chapter.

▼ *Status bar*. This shows information about your document, most of which you can ignore. For the most part, this book ignores it, too.

▼ *Scroll bars*. Chapter 2 covers these things, which help you move around in your document.

# Handy Guide to the Basic Mouse Maneuvers

If you're new to Windows, take a moment to look at the basic mouse maneuvers. Word for Windows is a heavy mouse user, despite years of

counseling, and this book assumes you're using the mouse to do stuff. (There are keyboard alternatives to some maneuvers, which are covered in the "Quick and Dirty Dozens" section at the end of this book.)

▼   *Point*—Move the mouse so that the on-screen pointer goes to something, such as a program icon.

▼   *Click*—Point to something and click the left mouse button. (Sometimes applications use the right mouse button for things, but this is rare.)

▼   *Double-click*—Point to something and click the left mouse button twice in rapid succession. If this doesn't work, double-click again, but leave less time between the two clicks.

▼   *Drag*—Point to something, hold down the left mouse button, and move the mouse. You'll "drag" whatever you've pointed to (as long as it is "draggable"). When you've dragged this thing to its destination, release the mouse button.

**TIP**

No one tells beginners this, but the instructions you'll read about Windows programs just assume you *know* that the left button is used 95 percent of the time. When you see an instruction that says, "Click the so-and-so icon," it means, "Move the mouse pointer to the so-and-so icon and click the *left* mouse button." When you see an instruction that says "Drag the icon to the such-and-such window, it means, "Move the mouse pointer to the icon, hold down the left mouse button, and move the icon to its destination."

# Handy Guide to Menus

If you're new to Windows, you should also note how to select a command. To open a menu, click on its name in the menu bar. A pull-down menu drops down. To select a command, click on it.

▼ For some commands, a dialog box appears that prompts you for more information about something. You choose options by clicking in the boxes, by choosing items from lists, or by typing in text areas. When you're finished choosing options, you can click OK to confirm your choices, or Cancel to exit without doing anything.

▼ To close a menu without selecting a command, click on the menu name again, or press the Esc key.

▼ Keyboard lovers can press the Alt key to activate the menu bar, then type the "key" (underlined) letter in the menu name to open the menu. To select a command, type the "key" (underlined) letter for that command.

▼ Word also offers keyboard shortcuts for some commands. And some buttons on the Toolbar are shortcuts for commands. The keyboard and Toolbar shortcuts are pointed out throughout this book.

# Entering Text (Thou shalt not press enter until...)

You've probably noticed the funny little black blinking bar. This is called the *insertion point*. It shows you where your text will appear when you start typing—so give it a try.

Go ahead, peck away, but remember one thing: *Don't press Enter* (that big key that would be the Return key on a typewriter). When you reach the end of a line, words that go over the margin are automatically "wrapped" down to the next line. This is called *word wrapping*. I don't think this is a typewriter anymore, Toto.

**TIP**

If you like to indent your paragraphs, press the Tab key to indent the first line. Don't enter the indentation with spaces. Never, never, indent with spaces, unless you want all the indents in your document to print with different indentation lengths (even though they all look the same on-screen). For more information on indenting with Word, flip to Chapter 13.

**Checklist**

▼ Press Enter *only* when you want to start a new paragraph.

▼ If you make a mistake while typing, press the Backspace key (the one with the left arrow, just above the Enter key) to rub out the error.

**"I HATE THIS!"**

## mY tEXT lOOKS lIKE tHIS!

If you see a bizarre capitalization pattern while you're typing, check to see whether the word CAPS appears on the status bar. Press the Caps Lock key to turn off the Caps Lock mode, which is causing the problem.

# Save It!

At this point, the text you've typed exists only in the computer's memory. That's necessary while you're working with the text, but it has one huge drawback: If the power goes bye-bye, your text does, too. (Your computer's memory can't hold text when the power's off.) To keep your text permanently, you must save it.

**BUZZWORDS**

**SAVE**

To transfer your work from your computer's memory to a disk, where it is "recorded" for permanent storage.

To save the document that's currently on-screen, click on **File** in the menu bar. Then click on the Save command. You see the Save As dialog box.

**TIP**

You can also click on the Save button in the Toolbar (this is the one with the little disk on it).

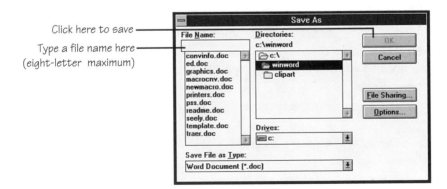

Click here to save

Type a file name here
(eight-letter maximum)

The only thing you need to do here is type a file name. This painful subject is explored in Chapter 5. For now, type a name using only alphabetical letters, and keep it to eight letters or less. (Don't type a period or an extension, even if you know what an "extension" is.) When you've finished typing the file name, click that big OK button, or just press Enter.

**"I HATE THIS!"**

### It says, "This is not a valid filename!"
Didn't listen to me, did you? Naughty, naughty. Maximum: eight characters. Use only alphabetical letters. Skip the period and three-letter extension. Click OK to continue, and retype the file name.

Next to appear is the Summary Info dialog box. The author's name is inserted automatically in the Author area. This name is the same one that you or somebody else typed when Word was installed. You can change it if it isn't correct, but first a message from your local computer nerd.

The Summary
Info dialog box

**TIP**

Always fill out Summary Info boxes! Doing so gives you the best chance of finding your file later, should you want to re-open it. This subject is explored in Chapter 19, *Where's My File?*

If you don't want to have to mess with the Summary Info box, here is how to keep Word from prompting you for it: Select **O**ptions from the **T**ools menu. Pick the Save icon from the scrolling box on the left. Uncheck the **P**rompt for Summary Info box.

To fill out the Summary Info dialog box, click within the Title area, and type a document title. Then press Tab and type a subject. Continue pressing Tab and typing stuff until you've filled out all the fields.

## Let's Get Out of Here

And now for your grand exit.

**TIP**

Never quit Word (or Windows) by just flipping off the power. There might be some work that's not saved. Even if you're sure you've saved everything, you must quit Word properly if you want the program to save choices you've made. Always quit properly.

To exit Word, move the pointer to the menu bar and click **F**ile. The File menu pops down. Now click Exit.

**"I HATE THIS!"**

## It's asking me whether I want to save changes!

Ah, you must have done something to your document after saving it—even something as harmless as pressing the space bar. If there have been any changes at all, Word won't let you quit without displaying this message. (This is really good, because you might have opened additional windows that aren't visible, and these windows might contain unsaved text.) To save your file, click the **Yes** button or just press Enter.

Now you're back to Program Manager. If you're done with Windows and your computer, you should exit Program Manager the same way you exited Word—click **File**, and then click Exit Windows. You see an alert box informing you that this will end your Windows session. To do so, just click OK or press Enter. When you see the C:\> thingie, you can turn off your computer.

# CHAPTER 2

# Editing
## (Slash-and-Burn Techniques)

## IN A NUTSHELL

▼ Open a document you previously saved
▼ Insert text within existing text
▼ Move around in your document
▼ Resave while you work
▼ Select text for editing
▼ Delete text
▼ Undo the deletion
▼ Copy and move text with the mouse
▼ Copy and move text with the Clipboard

From an author's standpoint, Ernest Hemingway had the ideal publication contract: It forbade his publisher to change a single word of his manuscripts. (This caused a certain amount of consternation at Scribner's when, long before such things became fashionable, he used a naughty word in a short story.) In truth, though, there aren't a lot of Hemingways around, and the rest of us hack writers really need to take a dispassionate second look at that first draft, the one that seemed so brilliant last night. Doesn't look so good in the cold light of day, does it? Darn.

Thanks to word processing technology, though, revision needn't be painful. With an easy mouse maneuver and the click of a key, a moronic word, sentence, or paragraph joins the ash heap of history. You can insert text as you please, and move text around until you've got it just right.

This chapter runs through the basics of editing with Word. Once again, many options and alternative ways of doing things aren't covered here—this chapter just boils it all down to the things people actually do when they edit with Word.

# Opening Documents (I *know* you're in there somewhere)

To work on a document you previously saved and closed, you *open* it. It's somewhere on that big hard disk, and you need to transfer it from the disk into the computer's memory, where you can work with it. Opening the document makes it available for editing.

**TIP**

Planning to open one of the last four documents you saved? If so, you're in luck. You can open it easily, just by choosing its name from the File menu. Click **File**, and look at the bottom area of the menu—you'll see the names of the last four documents you saved. To open one of them, just click the name, or type the number (**1**, **2**, **3**, or **4**) that precedes the name.

To open a document that isn't on the bottom of the File menu, move the mouse pointer to the menu bar and click **File**. When you see the File pull-down menu, click **Open**. You'll see the Open dialog box.

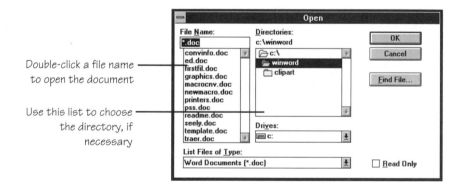

Double-click a file name to open the document

Use this list to choose the directory, if necessary

**TIP**

To display the Open dialog box super-fast, click the Open button on the Toolbar. It's the one with the arrow escaping from the file folder. If you don't see the Toolbar, open the **View** menu and choose **Toolbar**.

| Checklist |
|---|

▼ You'll see a lot of this Open dialog box. You use it every time you open a Word document that's not on the File menu.

▼ Under **D**irectories, you see the current directory. (A *directory* is a named section of your hard disk that has been set aside to store files of a certain type.) If your document is in some other directory, use the Directory list box to display this directory. If the directory concept is new to you, flip to Chapter 5.

▼ Look for your file in the list under the File **N**ame box. If you don't see it, click the down scroll arrow to bring more names into view. When you see your document's name, double-click it to open it. Word opens the document and puts it into a document window.

**"I HATE THIS!"**

### My document is gone!

Every computer user sings this lament sooner or later. If you're having trouble finding your document, be sure to check the File menu—if you recently saved your document, chances are it's listed there and you can retrieve it quickly just by clicking its name. Or turn to Chapter 19 to learn techniques for hunting the missing file.

# Inserting Text (Could you expand on that a little?)

One of the great things about word processing is that you can add text anywhere you like. This is great if sometimes you're in such a hurry to get things done that you leave out a crucial point.

To insert text within existing text, you begin by moving the *insertion point*—that blinking vertical line. Point somewhere with the *I-beam pointer*, and click the left mouse button. The I-beam pointer is a skinny, little thing—thin enough to let you slip it right between a couple of teensy characters. After you click, the insertion point magically appears where you pointed.

After moving the insertion point to a new location, you can type new text. Word pushes the existing text right and down, to make room. It's really easy to add text to your document. If you feel that a thought is missing or you didn't explain something well enough, move the insertion point and add a clarifying passage.

**"I HATE THIS!"**

### I tried to insert text, but it wiped out the text to the right!

If this happens, you somehow pressed the Ins (Insert) key. Doing so switches on the Overtype mode, one of Word's two text-entry modes. (A *mode* is an operating setting.) In the Overtype mode, the text you type wipes out existing text. You can tell when you're in the Overtype mode because OVR appears on the status bar (at the bottom of the Word window). To switch back to the Insert mode, in which you can insert text without disturbing existing text, just press the Ins key.

# Page Up, Page Down, Page All Around

If the text you want to edit isn't in view, you need to scroll the screen. Here's a quick overview of navigation techniques; flip to Chapter 6 for more about navigation.

▼   To scroll the screen down one line at a time, click the down scroll arrow. To scroll through several pages, drag the scroll box down. Click below the scroll box to scroll the screen one windowful at a time. To scroll back up, click the up scroll arrow, drag the scroll box back up, or click above the scroll box.

▼   You can also scroll down by pressing the PgDn key, and up by pressing the PgUp key.

**"I HATE THIS!"**

## I scrolled the screen, but it jumped back when I started typing!

When you scroll using the mouse and scroll bars, you don't move the insertion point. Suppose you scroll two or three pages and then start typing. The text you type is entered back where the insertion point is positioned! To prevent this from happening, click a new insertion point after scrolling.

# Resaving while You Work

Unless you want to lose all the hard work you've done, you need to save your work periodically. I recommend saving every five minutes or less. To resave your work, just click that cute little Save button on the Toolbar (it's the one that looks like a 3½-inch floppy disk, which doesn't make sense, because you're saving to your hard disk). Or you can click on **File** and then **Save**. Unlike the first time you save a file, you don't need to supply a file name. Word saves the file with the same name you used the first time.

# Selecting Text (Identify the victims)

Chances are, you're doing more drastic things to your document than just adding a little clarifying text here and there. Sometimes, even *I'd* like to get rid of an ill-considered word. Or an ill-chosen sentence. Or two. All right, I admit it, sometimes the whole darned page is ill-considered.

To get rid of large chunks of text, you need to *select* it. To select text means to highlight it on-screen, so that it appears in reverse video (white letters on a black background). Selecting is good for other things besides trashing text—it's also used for copying and moving the text, as you'll see later in this chapter, and for making it look pretty (the subject of Chapter 3).

In Word, selection techniques are as numerous as old friends after you've won the state lottery. You can select text in all kinds of different ways using the keyboard and the mouse. Your ever-faithful author has assembled the following list of most frequently used selection techniques:

---

**Checklist**

▼ The easiest way to select text is to drag over it. Move the pointer to the text you want to select, hold down the mouse button, and drag over the text. When you reach the end of the text you want to select, release the mouse button.

▼ To select a word, double-click it.

▼ To select an entire line, move the pointer to the left past the start of the line until the pointer changes from the I-beam to an arrow. Then click. (This area is called the *selection bar*.)

*continues*

▼   To select an entire paragraph, move the pointer to the selection bar and double-click.

▼   To select an entire document, move the pointer to the selection bar, hold down the Control (Ctrl) key, and click. Or press Ctrl and the 5 on the numeric keypad. (The numeric keypad is the set of numeric keys on the right side of your keyboard.)

▼   To select text with the keyboard, press and hold down the Shift key. Then use the arrow keys to highlight the text you want.

▼   To cancel the selection without doing anything drastic to the text, just click the insertion point anywhere within the document window (except within the selection).

# Deleting Text (Into the void...)

And now, let's get rid of the offending passage, the one that you've selected so carefully. The quickest, easiest, and niftiest way to obliterate the selection is just to type something new. The very first character you type wipes out the selection, and the rest of the text swarms in to fill in the gap. If you don't want to type something in the selected text's place, just press the Delete or Backspace key.

# Wait! It's All a Mistake! Bring It Back!

Just deleted the wrong thing, did you? Oops. *Don't type anything or choose any commands!* And don't panic! Click **Edit**, and choose **U**ndo. Alternatively, click the Undo button (it's the one with the little pencil

erasing something). (If you're keyboard-happy, you can press Ctrl+Z.) Presto! The selection pops back on-screen.

**TIP**

If you really did manage to wipe out much or all of your document, and Undo can't help, consider a maneuver called reverting to the last saved version. From the **File** menu, choose **C**lose. When you see the message *Do you want to save changes*, click **N**o. This abandons your changes, including the one in which you wiped out most of your text. Then re-open the last saved version; the stuff you deleted will be intact.

**CAUTION**

Be sure to choose Undo immediately after performing an unwanted command. If you wait and do something else, Word will undo the last thing you did—and that might not be the thing you want undone.

### To undo or not to undo

▼    You can tell when Undo can undo something. After performing an action, open the **E**dit menu and look at the **U**ndo option. If it says something like "Undo Cut" or "Undo Typing," you can undo your last action. If it's grayed and says "Can't Undo," well, that's pretty clear, isn't it?

▼    Generally, you can undo most editing changes, editing commands, and typing sprees (defined as the typing you did since you last moved the insertion point or chose a command). You can't undo file-related stuff, such as saving files or closing files with unsaved work.

*continues*

▼ If you choose Undo only to find that the command or action you performed was actually correct, you can undo what was undone: Just choose Undo Undo from the Edit menu. (I am *not* making this up.)

# Copying and Moving (Drag-and-drop)

Warm up your mouse, because you're about to learn the ultimate in mouse techniques: It's called *drag-and-drop*. The two basic drag-and-drop maneuvers are *copying* and *moving*.

First, select the text. To copy the selection, move the pointer *within* the selection, hold down the Ctrl key, and drag to where you want the copied text to appear. As you drag, notice that the pointer has changed shape slightly; there's a little box under it. This is intended to suggest that the pointer is carrying something. When you have moved this loaded pointer to where you want the copied text to appear, release the mouse button.

To move the selection, you do exactly the same thing, except you don't hold down the Ctrl key.

**TIP**

To copy or move to a part of the document that's not within the document window, just move the loaded pointer to the top or the bottom of the window. Word scrolls the screen in the indicated direction.

**"I HATE THIS!"**

### I tried to drag-and-drop, but it didn't work!

You need to activate drag-and-drop editing. From the Tools menu, choose Options. You see the Options dialog box, which lets you choose lots of options for the way Word works. Instead of bewildering yourself with zillions of options, though, just click the General icon in the Category list (at the left of the dialog box). In the Settings area, click the little check box next to Drag-and-drop Text Editing) so that an X appears in the check box. Then click the OK button (or just press Enter) to get back to your document. Now drag-and-drop should work just fine.

## Copying and Editing with the Clipboard

Drag-and-drop editing is the ultimate in editing maneuvers. But it only works within one window. If you try to drag some text to another document window, you'll quickly discover that it doesn't work. (Working with more than one document window is covered in Chapter 5.) In such situations, you'll have to resort to the old-fashioned Clipboard copying and moving techniques. If you're a mouse-hater, this method will suit your fancy better.

**BUZZWORDS**

**CLIPBOARD**

What's the Clipboard? It's a temporary storage area where Word parks text that you're copying or moving. The Clipboard can hold only one chunk of text at a time, though.

To copy or move text, you begin by selecting it. To copy the text, copy it to the Clipboard. Do so by clicking open the **E**dit menu and choosing **C**opy. Or, click the Copy button on the Toolbar. (This is the one with the two little pages right next to each other, next door to the scissors.)

To move the text, you begin by cutting it to the Clipboard. This deletes the text from its original location. Do so by clicking open the **E**dit menu and choosing **C**ut. Or, click the Cut button on the Toolbar. (This is the one with the little scissors.)

To put the copied or cut text in its new location, click the insertion point there. Then click open the **E**dit menu and choose **P**aste. You can also click the Paste button (This is the one that shows a little page falling off a Clipboard.)

---

**Checklist**

▼ If the whole thing was a huge mistake, click open the **E**dit menu and choose **U**ndo immediately.

▼ If you want to make multiple copies of the stuff that's in the Clipboard, just move the insertion point to new locations and choose **E**dit **P**aste (or click the Paste button) at each one.

---

**EXPERTS ONLY**

## Keyboard shortcuts for mouse haters

To copy text, select the text and then use Ctrl+C (hold down the Ctrl key, and while it's still being held down, press C or c—case doesn't matter). To cut text to the Clipboard, use Ctrl+X. To paste text from the Clipboard, use Ctrl+V.

## Top Ten Rejected Word for Windows Command Options

**10.** File Destroy

**9.** Lose Character

**8.** Insert Random Dialog from *Mary Worth* Comic Strip

**7.** Split Infinitive

**6.** Use the Power of the Dark Side of the Force

**5.** Translate to Klingon

**4.** Make It So

**3.** Window Break Pane

**2.** View Swimsuit Issue

**1.** Undo Undo Undo

# CHAPTER 3

# Formatting
## (The Beauty Shop)

## IN A NUTSHELL

▼ Emphasize words
▼ Change fonts
▼ Center, justify, and align text
▼ Adjust line spacing
▼ Repeat a format
▼ Add page numbers

Careful studies by crack business researchers have uncovered the real reason people are getting Word for Windows: Their co-workers are producing beautifully-formatted memos and reports, which subliminally manipulate the boss's brain. (The desired reaction: She looks up from the document and, with a zombie-like expression, says "This is *excellent* work. Here's a raise.") With this kind of competition, you just have to keep up.

This chapter focuses on the formatting maneuvers that 80 percent of Word users use 80 percent of the time. As for the other 20 percent, there's a 1,400-page book that's *just the thing* for them. They can read it while you vacation in a Caribbean island paradise.

# Be Emphatic!

Word has lots of character styles, including outline and cool-looking shadowed characters. But the most popular by far are **bold**, *italic*, and underline. Thanks to the Ribbon, these forms of character emphasis are only a click away.

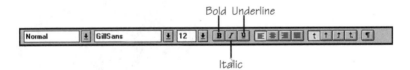

First, select the text. (For the lowdown on selection, flip to "Selecting Text" in Chapter 2. Then do one of the following: To boldface the text, click the Bold button (**B**). To italicize the text, click the Italic button (*I*). To underline the text, click the Underline button (u).

**Checklist**

▼    If you want to create an emphasis that really looks obnoxious, you can apply two or all three of these to the same text.

▼    If the emphasis doesn't look good, you can get rid of it. From the **E**dit menu, select **U**ndo. Or select the text again, and click the same button you used to apply the emphasis. This time, it goes away.

▼    If you threw caution to the wind and applied more than one emphasis, you can get rid of all of them by selecting the text and pressing Ctrl+space bar.

**TIP**

To enter text with bold, italic, or underline, position the insertion point where you want the text to start. Then, click the button you want (Bold, Italic, or Underline). Then type. When you get tired of the emphasis you chose, click the button again to return to the normal (unemphasized) style.

**TIP**

Keyboard lovers can select the text and then press Ctrl+B for bold, Ctrl+I for italic, or Ctrl+U for underline.

# Look Your Best (Dress up in the latest font)

Another formatting change that will make your document shake, rattle, and roll is a font change.

**BUZZWORDS**

**FONT**

A distinctive typeface design that has a name, such as Helvetica or Times Roman.

Fonts have creative names that don't tell you much about them; you're just supposed to *know*. Here are some examples:

**Bodoni**

Helvetica

Times Roman

**Garamond Condensed**

Courier

San Francisco

**Checklist**

▼ Your system is probably equipped with several fonts. You can buy additional fonts if you want.

▼ There are two basic kinds of fonts, *serif* and *sans-serif*. Serif fonts (such as Times Roman) have those cute little finishing strokes at the end of each part of the character. Sans-serif fonts (such as Helvetica) don't have the little serif thingies.

▼ Font designs convey a subtle message. New Century Schoolbook says, "Let's get serious. Study this." Garamond says, "This is worth reading, but for heaven's sake, lighten up and enjoy life." Times Roman says, "This is the news from an authoritative source." Helvetica says, "Aren't we modern?"

▼ Generally, you use serif fonts for body text (the paragraphs of your document). If you use sans-serif fonts, you should use them for titles and headings.

▼ Using more than two fonts in a document is considered to be about as dorky as wearing white socks with black shoes.

▼ Font sizes are measured in *points*, of which there are a stunning 72 to the inch. A font that is 12 points high gives you six lines of text to the inch, which is standard for typescript. Books and magazines usually use 9- or 10-point fonts. Headings and titles use bigger fonts, such as 18 or 24 points. A title looks *really* big in a 60-point font.

---

The easiest way to choose fonts is to use the Ribbon, the bar below the Toolbar. (If you don't see the Ribbon, click open the **View** menu and choose **Ribbon**.) From the Ribbon, you can choose the font, the font and the font size, or just the size.

**1.** Select the text first.

**2.** Move the pointer to the *second* text box on the ribbon, which probably says something like *Courier* or *Arial*. Click the underlined arrow. To see more font names, click the down arrow on the scroll bar. When you see the name of a font you want, click its name.

**3.** If you want to choose the font size, too, click the down arrow in the font size box (the next one on the right of the font box), and click the point size you want. Or, just double-click the current font size, type a new font size, and press Enter.

If the font and font size choices prove disastrous, click open the **Edit** menu and choose **Undo** immediately.

**TIP**

To change the font throughout your document, select your entire document by moving the mouse pointer to the selection bar (the left border along the text), holding down the Ctrl key, and clicking the left mouse button. (Or press Ctrl and 5 on the numeric keypad. Then choose the font and/or font size.

## Top Ten Rejected Font Names

**10.** IRS Tax Form Gothic

**9.** Being Of Sound Mind (wills only)

**8.** USDA "Choice" Block Letter Bold (requires steak printer)

**7.** Lawyerly Extra Fine Squint-to-See-It Font

**6.** Klingon PlasmaBolt Bold (shields up)

**5.** Gang Territory SprayPaint Italic (outdoor use only; high-caliber automatic weapon strongly suggested)

**4.** Physician Prescription Script (illegible)

**3.** Publisher's Clearinghouse "You May Have Already Won" Ultra (large font sizes only)

**2.** Ayatollah Calligraphic Death Threat Condensed (requires hostage)

**1.** New *Enquirer* Roman (requires only a third-grade education)

# Centering, Justifying, and Other Misalignments

As you enter text with Word, the program uses its default alignment: flush left. The term *alignment* refers to the way the margin is evened, or aligned. There are four kinds of alignments, easily accessible from the Ribbon: flush left, centered, flush right, and justified.

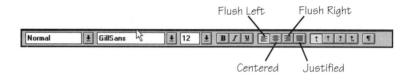

In flush left alignment, all the lines are pushed up flush against the left margin, but no attempt is made to even the right margin. Flush left text is unpretentious. Modest. It doesn't call attention to itself. It's easy to read. Few computer users are content with flush left alignment, though. They want their text to look like a printed magazine or book, with both margins even, in the vain hope that this will give them a psychological edge over the reader.

In centered alignment, the text is automatically positioned in the center of the page. Centered text is useful for titles and document headings.

Flush right alignment is an amusing, but seldom-used, alternative to flush left alignment, in which the right margin is nice and straight, whereas the left one is left all ragged, jumbled, and uneven. This is generally used only for *epigrams*, those intelligent sayings of intelligent people which you place at the beginning of a document in the earnest hope that doing so will make the author look intelligent.

And here it is: *justification*, so called because it helps to justify why you spent all that money on your computer. In justified alignment, both of the margins are even. This isn't an easy thing to do, and it keeps your computer busy thinking about where it's going to put all those little spaces so that each line is even. If you're using really narrow margins, Word may not do a very good job at this, resulting in big, ugly gaps between words.

## Deciding on an Alignment

Here's how to choose alignments:

**1.** Select the text. If you're selecting just one paragraph, it's enough to park the insertion point within it—you don't actually have to highlight the whole thing.

**2.** Click one of the alignment buttons on the Ribbon. The text you've selected jumps this way or that, depending on which alignment you chose.

If you're not happy with your alignment choice, just click a different one while the text is still selected.

**TIP**

The Ribbon shows the alignment that's currently in effect, and that's the one that Word will use as you type text. To change the alignment, click one of the alignment buttons and then type away. The alignment you choose remains in effect until you change it.

"I HATE THIS!"

## My alignment choice disappeared!

You're editing, right? And what's more, you were editing something at the end of a paragraph. Here's what happened: You accidentally deleted the hidden *paragraph mark*, which Word enters every time you press Enter. Without going into the details, you can think of this little hidden thing as the place where paragraph formats (such as alignment) are stored. If you delete it, you lose the format. The cure: Undo immediately (click open the **E**dit menu and choose **U**ndo, or click the Undo button). If you've already done something else and can't undo the deletion, place the insertion point where the paragraphs should break, and press Enter. Then place the insertion point in the paragraph that lost its format, and repeat the formatting command. For the lowdown on paragraph marks, see "12 Naughty Things You Really Shouldn't Do" in the *Quick and Dirty Dozens* section at the end of the book.

## How Not to Indent

If you want to indent a paragraph, don't indent with the space bar. The text might not line up with other indentations when you print.

## How to Indent

If you want to indent the first line of every paragraph, press Tab. If you want to indent all lines, you can use the Toolbar. Two of the buttons on the Toolbar enable you to indent (and unindent) text quickly. They're called Nest Paragraph and Unnest Paragraph.

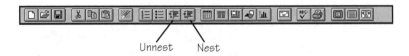

Unnest    Nest

To indent a paragraph one-half inch, just place the insertion point in the paragraph and click Nest Paragraph. To indent it more, click Nest Paragraph again. If you indented too much, click Unnest Paragraph. If you keep clicking Unnest Paragraph, the paragraph winds up against the left margin again.

CAUTION

You might think that you can click the left alignment button to undo an indent, but you can't. You have to undo the indent.

# Line Spacing (Drawing a blank)

By default, Word uses single line spacing. However, you can use Ctrl+O (the letter) so that Word automatically adds a blank line before each paragraph. When you press Enter, Word enters a nice, blank line. This is really cool for lots of writing tasks, such as letters and memos.

"I HATE THIS!"

### I can't get rid of this blank line!

If you've pressed Ctrl+O and you're typing away, Word enters a blank line every time you press Enter. To get rid of it, place the insertion point in the paragraph (or select two or more paragraphs) and press Ctrl+0 (the number, not the letter). That's right, Ctrl+zero. To remember the difference, use this handy memory aid: "**O**h my, blank lines fly, zer**O** comes by, blank lines die."

If you like, you can change the line spacing. The easiest way to do so is to use keyboard commands. To double-space your text, select it and press Ctrl+2. To restore single spacing, press Ctrl+1. If you want space-and-a-half lines, press Ctrl+5 (don't blame me, I didn't make these up).

**TIP**

Key combinations in this book are indicated with a plus (+) sign. Press and hold down the first key. Then press the second key. Release both keys.

# Repeating a Format

A very handy but seldom-used Word command is the **R**epeat option on the **E**dit menu. This option repeats the last command or typing you did. Suppose you selected some text and chose a font for it. You want to do the same thing somewhere else. If you select the next block of text, you can just choose **R**epeat instead of going through all the anguish of choosing the font again. To repeat your last action, open the **E**dit menu and choose **R**epeat.

**TIP**

A useful keyboard shortcut (a rare thing in Word) is F4, which is the same as choosing **R**epeat from the **E**dit menu.

**I HATE WORD FOR WINDOWS!**

**Checklist**

▼ Like Undo, Repeat tells you when it can repeat something—and what it can repeat. After performing an action, open the **E**dit menu and look at the **R**epeat option. If it says something like "Repeat Cut" or "**R**epeat Typing," you can repeat your last action. If it's grayed and says "Can't Repeat," you'll have to choose the command again the same way you chose it the first time.

▼ Generally, you can repeat most editing changes, editing commands, and typing sprees (defined as the typing you did since you last moved the insertion point or chose a command). You can't repeat file-related stuff, such as saving files or closing files with unsaved work.

**EXPERTS ONLY**

### Copy cat

Let's say you've created a nice format somewhere in your document. The emphasis? Italic. The font? Arial. The size? 72 points. Now you want to use this same collection of formats somewhere else. Does this mean you have to choose all those commands all over again? Nope, because you can copy formats.

First, select the text you want to format. Then, to copy character formats (fonts, font sizes, and so on), move the mouse pointer to the text that has the format you want to copy. Hold down the Ctrl and Shift keys. With both held down, click the left mouse button. Lo and behold! The selected text takes on the formats of the text you clicked.

To copy *paragraph* formats (such as alignment, line spacing, and indents), move the mouse pointer to the *selection bar* (the blank area just to the left of the text) next to text that has the format you want to copy. Hold down the Ctrl and Shift keys. With both held down, click the left mouse button. Double Lo and behold! The selected text takes on the format of the paragraphs you clicked next to.

# Adding Page Numbers

Any document more than one page long really should have page numbers. These can really prove helpful as the poor reader tries to keep the pages in order. To add page numbers to your document, do this:

1. From the Insert menu, choose Page Numbers. You'll see the Page Numbers dialog box.

2. In the Position area, choose where you want the page numbers to print by clicking the little round things (these are called *option buttons*).

3. In the Alignment area, choose where you want the page numbers to appear in the top or bottom margin (flush to the left margin, in the center, or flush to the right margin).

4. Click OK, or just press Enter, to confirm your choice.

Word prints the page numbers on all the pages except page 1. (You usually don't want a page number on page 1.)

**"I HATE THIS!"**

### I don't see any page numbers!

You won't, either, until you print your document or look at it in Print Preview, discussed in the next chapter. But they're there. Relax.

# CHAPTER 4

# Printing
## (Get It Down in Black and White)

## IN A NUTSHELL

- ▼ View a preview of your document's printed pages
- ▼ Solve page break problems
- ▼ Print your document quickly
- ▼ Print your document with options

Chances are pretty good that your document's destined for the printed page, unless you've taken a frank look at your document and decided Not To Publish. If "print" it shall be, you're in for a bout with your printer, yet another of those vexing hardware components that always seems ready to cause problems.

This chapter looks at printing with Word, a process that ought to be simple. And, sometimes it is. But you have to realize what's going on when you print. Remember, your document isn't really in pages—it's a long, shelf-paper-like scroll, and Word has to partition it into pages before printing can occur. Sometimes Word doesn't do this in a pleasing way, so it's wise to take a look at the page breaks (the places Word proposes to break pages) before printing. What's more, the printer can cause problems of its own, which you can deal with using the various clever tricks discussed in this chapter. If these do not work, try beating it repeatedly with a blunt object.

**TIP**

This chapter assumes that you've set up your printer with Windows, and that everything's hunky-dory between these two irritable components of your system. If you think there's been a separation or argument, or (worse) if the two have never met, get a Windows wizard to set up your printer for you.

# Print Preview (Sneak a peek)

In the default (Normal) view you see on-screen, Word displays much of what will appear when printed, such as character emphases (bold, italic, and underline), fonts, indents, line spacing, alignment, and more. (You can see even more formats in the Page Layout view, discussed in Chapter 11. If you're looking at your document on a standard 13- or 14-inch

monitor, though, it's hard to see what the whole page will look like. That's a job for Print Preview.

To display your document in Print Preview, place the insertion point on the page you want to see. (If you forget to do this, don't worry; you can page around once you're in Print Preview.) Then open the File menu and click Print Preview (Alt+F, V). Print Preview reveals itself.

The Print
Preview screen

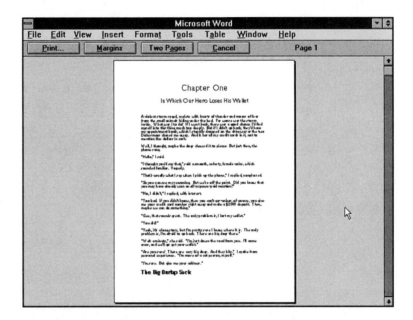

▼   If you see a single-page display, you can click the Two Pages button to see a two-page display.

▼   To view other pages, press PgDn and PgUp, or click the up or down arrows on the scroll bar.

*continues*

▼ In Print Preview, you are looking for any kind of obvious format-ting problem, such as forgetting to center a heading. But more than anything, you're looking for the *bad page break*. The preceding figure shows a classic example of a page break gone awry: a heading positioned all by itself at the bottom of the page.

▼ Why do bad page breaks occur? Murphy's Law, section WP-1131 ("A document subheading tends to gravitate toward the bottom of the page, so that it appears by itself.")

▼ To exit Print Preview, click Cancel or just press Esc. You'll see your document again. If everything looked hunky-dory, skip to the "Printing" section later in this chapter.

# Punishing Bad Page Breaks

If you're reading this, your Print Preview revealed a heading or title posi-tioned at the bottom of the page, no doubt, and you're wondering how to fix it. Don't feel bad; this is a really common error. If you look around at the word-processed documents in your life, I'll bet you find it after looking at only two or three of them.

You can fix this bad page break problem in two ways: the bad way and the good way.

## The Bad Way

The bad way to fix page break problems is to insert a hard page break. In a hard page break, you tell Word, in effect, "Break this page here, no

matter what." Admittedly, there are sometimes good reasons to insert a hard page break. For example, suppose you want your document to have a title page, all by itself. To get Word to start the text on a new page, you shouldn't press the Enter key a zillion times until a new page starts; you should use a hard page break. So, I'll tell you how to do it. Just don't use this procedure to fix the heading-at-the-bottom-of-the-page problem.

To insert a hard page break, press Ctrl+Enter. Word breaks the page at the insertion point's location. On-screen (in Normal view), a hard page break looks much like a soft page break, except that the dots are closer together.

**TIP**

What's bad about a hard page break? Suppose you use a hard page break to deal with the heading-at-the-bottom-of-the-page problem. OK, fine, that fixes it—the heading prints at the top of the next page. But what happens if you later add or delete text above the hard page break? Word still breaks the page where you indicated, resulting (probably) in a lot of blank space at the bottom of one of the pages. This looks ugly. When people read your document, they will say, "Tsk, tsk. Bad page break." And this is just what you were trying to avoid!

If you want to get rid of a hard page break, you can. Just place the insertion point on it and press Del.

## The Good Way

The good way to fix page break problems is to format the heading (the one at the bottom of the page) with the Keep With Next option. This

option, buried deep within the Paragraph dialog box, tells Word, "Don't break a page after this text." This option comes into play only if Word is contemplating a page break at that exact spot. Otherwise, it's ignored. This prevents a bad page break from occurring if you subsequently add or delete text above the heading.

To format a heading with the Keep With Next option, try this:

**1.** Place the insertion point within the heading's text.

**2.** Open the Format menu and choose **P**aragraph (Alt+T, P). You see the Paragraph dialog box, which has about one million options. You can ignore all of them for now except Keep With **N**ext.

**3.** Move the pointer to the Keep With **N**ext check box and click the left mouse button. You should see an X in the check box. If not, click it again.

**4.** Click OK or just press Enter.

This solves the problem (without causing new ones).

# Printing

If your document looks OK in Print Preview (or if you don't give a darn what it looks like in Print Preview), try printing.

**TIP**

> Before your final printout, get Word to proof your document. For more information, see Chapter 8, "Proofing Text."

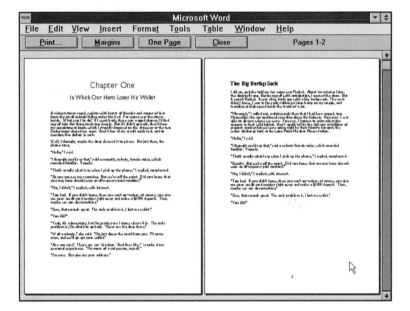

Two-page Print
Preview with
page break
problem solved.

To print, your printer must be "on-line" or "selected" (ready to receive stuff from the computer). This is usually the case, but you should check to make sure. Look on your printer for a button called On Line or Select. This button probably has an indicator light. When it's on, the printer is ready to go. If it's off, press the button to turn on the light.

**"I HATE THIS!"**

## On Line, Off Line, Out of Line

Why would someone have turned off the On Line button? With most printers, you have to take the computer *off line* (a techie expression that means *break the connection*) to advance the paper. Most printers have Line Feed and Form Feed buttons that advance the paper one line or one page at a time, respectively. If the printer's off line, it's probably because someone wanted to eject a page.

When your printer is on and selected, just click the Print tool (it's the one with the printer on it). You see a message that Word is printing your document. Then—with luck—things start happening at the printer.

"I HATE THIS!"

## Help! I got an error message!

Is the printer on? Is the printer selected (on-line)? Is there a cable between the printer and the computer? Is there paper in the printer? Is there a user at the keyboard? Is the user reading a Harlequin romance again instead of reading about the Print command in Word for Windows?

If you've checked all the obvious stuff and your printer still doesn't work, don't torture yourself—get help from someone who knows this system. That's especially true if you're using a printer that's on a network. Almost always, you have to do something unusual to get network printers to respond.

### Top Ten Rejected Printer Names

**10.** Rat-a-Tat Data Banger

**9.** Jam-O-Matic

**8.** TonerEater XL

**7.** Page-A-Day Special

**6.** Jiffy Jammer II

**5.** Document Donkey

**4.** Presto Paper Pappy

**3.** Tree Eater/Lumber Nibbler (tie)

**2.** Pulp Stainer Deluxe

**1.** SpatterJet 500

**"I HATE THIS!"**

### It doesn't have quite the look I wanted!

Rare is the printout that looks good on the first try.

Forget to add page numbers? Flip to "Adding Page Numbers" in Chapter 3.

Some text doesn't have the right font? Flip to "Look Your Best (Dress up in the latest font)" in Chapter 3.

More character emphasis than you bargained for? Bold barging in where it shouldn't? Italic itching to take over your document? Underline unmasking itself in new, unexpected situations? Flip to "Be Emphatic!" in Chapter 3, where the secrets of canceling character emphases are disclosed.

# Picky Printing

If you want to refine the printing process—print only certain pages, print multiple copies—you can do so. With Word, you can choose lots of print options using the Print dialog box. Open the **File** menu and choose **Print** (Alt+F, P).

▼ To print more than one copy of your document, click the up arrow in the Copies box. This raises the number in the text box. (We nerds like to say that it *increments* the number.) If you raise it too much, click the down arrow, which—you guessed it—*decrements* the number.

▼ To print just the current page, click the big, round O next to Current Page.

▼ To print a range of pages, click the O next to Pages. Type a beginning page number in the From box and an ending page number in the To box. To type in these boxes, just click within the box and type a number. If you don't type a number in the To box, Word starts printing on the From page and continues until it reaches the end of your document or the end of time, whichever comes first.

▼ If you're printing more than one copy of a document, you might want to click the Collate Copies check box. This tells Word to print one complete copy of a document before printing the next copy. Otherwise, Word prints all the page 1s, followed by all the page 2s, and so on, forcing you to do the collating by hand. Note, however, that it takes longer to print this way. If this option is grayed, it means your printer can't collate the copies, so forget the whole thing or get a new printer.

▼ To print, click OK.

▼ If your printer is up to the task, you can get Word to print envelopes. For information, see Chapter 12.

**EXPERTS ONLY**

## Read this if you're dying to know what the Options button does

You've probably noticed that big Options button in the Print dialog box. If you click it, you see the Options dialog box, which lists the printing options you can choose. One of the options I especially like is **R**everse Print Order, which starts printing from the last page instead of the first. For my printer, this is great because otherwise I have to put all the pages in order manually. Another great option: Click the **S**ummary Info box to get Word to print the Summary Info automatically (Summary Info is discussed in Chapter 1). When you're finished choosing options, click OK.

# PART II

# Be Your Own Editor

**Includes:**

# CHAPTER 5

# Managing Documents
## (What's Up, DOC?)

## IN A NUTSHELL

▼ Open a document on
   another disk

▼ Understand what all this
   "directory" nonsense
   means

▼ Open a document in a
   different directory

▼ Save a file to a different
   name, directory, or disk

▼ Work with two or more
   documents at a time

▼ Split one document into
   two windows

This chapter surveys document-management stuff that you might need to do from time to time as you edit Word documents. For example, you learn how to open a document that's in a different directory, as well as how to work with two or more documents at a time. It isn't really meant to be read at one sitting, as if there were going to be a quiz at the end. When you need some of the information in this chapter, just look it up.

# Opening a Document on Another Disk

Say your friend wants you to edit his Great American Novel. He gives you a copy of the document files on disk. How can you open them? If you want to open a file that's on a floppy disk, you use the Open dialog box to select a different drive. First, figure out what a drive is. Then figure out how to get at stuff on disks in that drive.

**Drivel on Drives**

▼ If you have one floppy disk drive, this drive is called drive A.

▼ If you have two floppy disk drives, the one on the top is probably drive A, and the one on the bottom is drive B.

▼ Very few people have turned their computers upside down, so it's unlikely that drive A is on the bottom. If you have turned your computer upside down, though, you can perform the following procedure with no trouble if you do a headstand.

Here's how to retrieve a file from a floppy disk in drive A or B:

**1.** Click open the File menu and choose **Open**, or just click the Open tool. You see the Open dialog box.

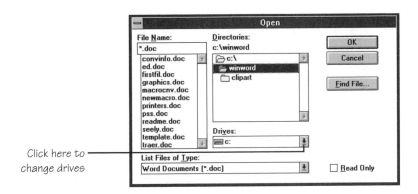

Click here to change drives

**2.** Put the disk in the drive.

**3.** Click the underlined arrow next to the Drives box. You see a list of the drives on your system.

**4.** Click the drive you want to open (drive A or B). Word tries to find Word documents on this disk. If there are any, you see their names in the File **N**ame list.

**5.** Click on the file you want to open.

**6.** Choose OK to open the file.

**"I HATE THIS!"**

## It says, "System Error—Cannot Read from Drive A" (or B)!

Make sure the disk is pushed in all the way. If it's a 5 ¼-inch disk, make sure the drive door is latched. Now click **R**etry. If this still doesn't work, there's something wrong with the disk—maybe it's a Macintosh disk, or maybe it's not formatted, or maybe somebody took it with them in the bathtub or used it as a beer coaster. Press Cancel to give up, and try another disk.

**EXPERTS ONLY**

### File conversion for the criminally curious

In the file list, Word lists only .DOC files—documents created by Word for Windows. You can open documents that were created by another word processor. First display all files: Click the down arrow next to List Files of **T**ype, and choose All Files (*.*). This option lists all the files on the disk, no matter what program created them. Then select the file you want. Word guesses what program created it—usually it's right. Click on OK, and Word opens the file.

## Directory Assistance (411)

A directory is a section of your hard disk that has been set aside for storing files of like type, such as all the letters you've written to your boss over the years asking for a raise. Chances are, you're working with a hard disk big enough to hold tens of thousands of files—and somehow, they've got to be organized. It makes a lot of sense to keep files of like type in their own area. And that's just what directories are for.

**BUZZWORDS**

**DIRECTORY**

A section of your hard disk that has been set aside for storing files of certain type (such as recipes or Word program files).

With Windows, you can think of directories as if they were file folders, each of which can contain files (documents stored on disk) as well as

more file folders. Here's a visual representation of what your hard disk's directory structure might look like:

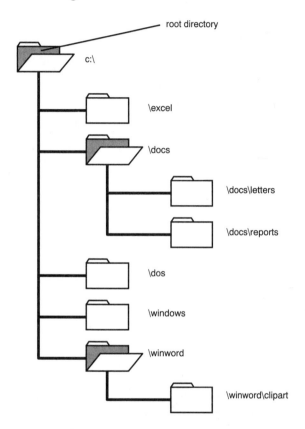

root directory

c:\

\excel

\docs

\docs\letters

\docs\reports

\dos

\windows

\winword

\winword\clipart

**Checklist**

▼ The root directory is the "top" folder from which all the other directories branch out. The root directory, poor thing, doesn't get to have a name; it's indicated only by a solitary backslash, plus the drive name (c:\).

*continues*

I HATE WORD FOR WINDOWS!

▼ Every directory can have directories within it. In this tree, the root directory has five directories: \excel, \docs, \dos, \windows, and \winword. The directory \docs has directories within it, called \docs\letters and \docs\reports. The directory \winword (Word's directory) has one directory within it: \winword\clipart. Your disk probably has different directories within the root directory, but it's a safe bet that \winword is among them (unless you're just reading this book to imagine what working with Word would be like).

▼ When a directory is open (like \winword, in the picture on the preceding page), the little folder picture is open, and you see the directories within them. Closed directories might have directories within them, too, but you can't see them when they're closed.

▼ You can open a folder by double-clicking it.

▼ You may have the term *subdirectories* thrust at you. What are *subdirectories*? Basically, they are the same as directories. Sometimes this term is used to talk about the relation between two directories. When a directory is placed within another directory, like \clipart within \winword, the one that's *within* is called a subdirectory. Technically, though, all directories are subdirectories of the root directory. The bottom line is that the terms *subdirectory* and *directory* mean the same thing.

**TIP**

Get your local Windows genius to create a directory called c:\docs, which you can use to store your Word documents. While you're at it, ask for a slight modification to the Windows program icon's properties—a modification that will make this new directory the default one for file saving and file opening operations. The standard payment for this operation is a

cold Jolt cola and a bag of Cheetos, although the precise level of compensation in your area may vary depending on local market factors.

# Opening Documents in Another Directory

Here's your problem. You or someone else saved a document in a directory other than Word's. As a result, it doesn't show up in the Open dialog box's file list. You have to change directories to open the file. You do this by using the Directories list box in the Open dialog box.

**TIP**

Suppose you're in a big, deep, hole in the ground, and you want to get into another big, deep, hole in the ground, next door. To do so, you have to climb to the surface. The same goes for directories. If you're in the \winword directory, you have to go back up to the root directory before you can go back down into another one.

Here's how to open a file in a different directory.

1. Double-click the root directory symbol (c:\). This takes you out of Word's directory and back up to the surface level. Now the Directories list shows all the directories off the root. These are shown as folders.

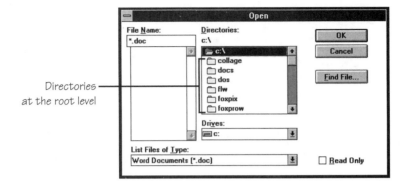

Directories at the root level

**2.** Double-click the name of the folder that you want to open. Look for your file in the file name list, to the left.

**3.** If the file isn't in this directory, you have two options. You could open any folders within this directory (go deeper into the pit). To do so, double-click the folder you want to open. Or you can climb back up to the surface. To do this, double-click on the root directory.

**4.** When you see your file in the file list, double-click the file name to open the file.

"I HATE THIS!"

## I've been clicking these folders for hours and I *still* can't find my #$#%$& file!

Don't despair—and please, don't put your fist through the monitor—because help is on the way. Flip to Chapter 19.

# Saving to a Different Name, Directory, or Disk

When you save a document the first time, you see the Save As dialog box. You give the document a name, and you save it. Subsequently, you don't see the Save As dialog box when you save—Word just saves the document using the current name and location. If you want to save the document with a new name or a different location, you must conjure up the Save As dialog box again and change the settings.

**TIP**

Floppy disks are cheap—your time isn't. Every time you create a valuable file, make a copy of it on a floppy disk, using the procedure discussed here. Better yet, back up all your work regularly using a backup utility program.

Follow these steps:

**1.** Click open the File menu and click Save As.

**2.** Do one of the following:

To change the name of the document, type a new name in the File Name text box. Type no more than eight letters, and don't use spaces or punctuation. Don't use a period or an extension (like .TXT or .YUK). If you omit the period and extension, Word automatically supplies the default .DOC extension, which is good, because Word needs this extension to help you hunt down and retrieve your Word documents.

To save the document to a new directory, double-click the root directory symbol (in the directories list) to show the top-level directories. Then double-click the name of the directory in which you want to save the document.

To save the document to a floppy disk, put the disk in the drive. Then click the down arrow next to the Drives list box, and choose the drive you want from the list.

**3.** Click OK or just press Enter.

After you save the document to a new name or location, Word retains the original copy as it was the last time you saved it.

**EXPERTS ONLY**

### Sharing files with Non-Word Users

Do you need to give your document to someone who uses a different word processing program—say, WordPerfect? Click open the Save File as Type list box and choose WordPerfect 5.0 or WordPerfect 5.1. Word will save your document in WordPerfect format, retaining all the formats you have chosen. You can also save your file to a format that is readable by the Macintosh version of Microsoft Word, in case you have to give your disk to a Mac user. (Macs have cunning little disk drives that can read your 3 ½-inch disks.)

# Working with Two or More Documents

Often, it's cool to work with two or more documents. Suppose that in your last letter to your boss, you developed a really superb argument for why you deserve a raise. Now, in your new letter, you want to use the same argument, but with a clever variation you just thought up. If you open the previous letter, you can copy part of it to the new document you're creating, reducing the amount of typing you have to do.

When you open a second document, whether it's a new one or an existing one you retrieved, it goes into a separate window. You may or may not be able to see both windows, depending on the size of the window. If the second document window is *maximized*, or bigger than the first document window, you won't see the first window.

**BUZZWORDS**

### MAXIMIZED WINDOW

*A maximized window* is enlarged so that it fills the entire screen. To maximize a window, click the Maximize button ▲ in the top right corner.

**TIP**

Here's something awesome. Click open the **W**indow menu and choose **A**rrange All. Word automatically sizes the windows so that you can see both of them. To zoom one of the windows to full size, click the Maximize button (the "up" button on the right edge of the title bar); click it again to restore the window to half-screen size. To use the other window, just click in it.

### Basic window maneuvers with Word

▼ Only one window is editable at a time. This window, called the *active window*, has a dark title bar and all the scroll bar junk.

▼ To activate the other window, just click in it. If you can't see it, click open the **W**indow menu, and look at the bottom of the menu—you'll see a list of all the open windows. Just click the name of the window you want to see.

*continues*

▼ To size a window, move the pointer to one of the corners. When you see a diagonal arrow with two heads, click and drag the pointer. If you see a dragon with three eyes, call a doctor.

▼ To close a file, click open the **File** menu and choose **Close**. Or, just double-click the window's Control menu box (the one at the top left corner of the window with the dash in it). When prompted to save your work, answer Yes, No, or Cancel.

Click here to
maximize the
window

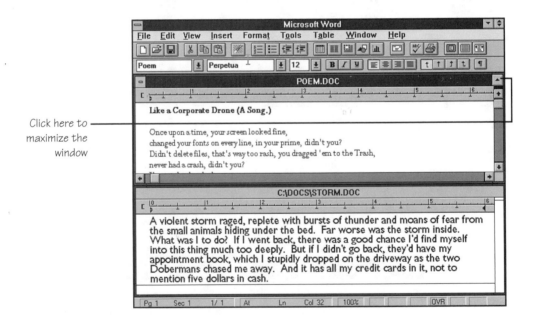

# Splitting One Document into Two Windows

With Word, you can open two (or more) separate windows on the same document, or you can split a window into two *panes*, each of which can show a different part of the same document. Why would you want to do

this? Well, suppose you're editing. In an introductory paragraph, you make big promises to your reader about what's going to be covered. To make sure you cover all the topics you promised you'd cover, you can keep this paragraph in view while you're editing the body text.

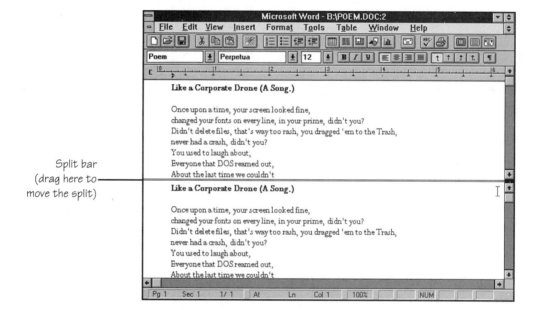

Split bar (drag here to move the split)

▼ To open a new window on a document at any time, just click open the **W**indow menu and choose **N**ew Window. Word opens a new window on the same document, titled with the same name. However, the name is followed by a colon and the number 2 (as in `Microsoft Word - C:\DOCS\POEM.DOC:2`). The original window is titled with number 1. You switch between these windows just like you switch between windows that contain different documents.

*continues*

**Checklist, continued**

▼  To split the window into two panes, move the pointer to the split bar—a little black rectangle that's right on top of the up scroll arrow (on the vertical scroll bar to the right of the screen). Double-click the split bar to split the screen in half. Or, you can single-click and drag to make the window the size you want.

▼  After you split the window into two panes, each pane has its own scroll bars, so you can scroll them independently—when you scroll one pane, the other stays put.

▼  To move the split, move the pointer to the split bar again, and position the pointer over the split bar until it changes shape (you'll see a bar with arrows pointing up and down). Then drag the split bar up or down.

▼  To get rid of the split, just double-click the split bar again or drag it to above the up scroll arrow.

# CHAPTER 6
# More Editing Stuff

## IN A NUTSHELL

▼ Find out which page you're on
▼ Go to a page number you specify
▼ Go back to your previous editing location
▼ View the page layout
▼ Display paragraph marks
▼ Use special hyphens and dashes

I HATE WORD FOR WINDOWS!

Word provides plenty of tools for helping you edit your document, but there's no need to study them all as if graduation depended on it. Some of the stuff in this chapter may prove helpful to you, particularly if you work with documents several pages or more in length. Also worth looking at is the stuff about those mysterious paragraph marks. Every Word user, sooner or later, has to cope with these things.

The sections of this chapter aren't meant to be read in order like your organic chemistry textbook. Just take a look at any section that seems to contain useful information.

# Where Am I?

An early U.S. aviator named Douglas Corrigan (known to history as Wrong-Way Corrigan) departed New York City one foggy morning in 1927, ostensibly bound for Los Angeles, California—and without a compass. Corrigan landed 23 hours later in Dublin, Ireland. When told where he was, Corrigan exclaimed, "I flew the wrong way!"

Deep in the depths of editing a Word document, you might feel that same Corrigan-like disorientation. That little one-third-of-a-page document window doesn't give you much of a clue about your surroundings. But Word gives you a clue.

Look at the page number indicator, a boxy area on the left side of the status bar (at the bottom of the screen). Chances are, it says something like Pg 2  Sec 1 2/2. This means the insertion point is currently located on page 2. Just ignore the Sec 1 part for now. The third indicator, 2/2, tells you the current page number *and* the total number of pages in the document.

## Go To

The Go To command enables you to jump quickly to the beginning of a page you specify. To use Go To, press the F5 key. At the bottom of the screen, you will see the message Go To, followed by the insertion point. Type the number of the page to which you want to jump. Then press Enter.

## Take It from the Beginning (Or, the end is near)

Want to scroll quickly to the beginning of the document or go to the end? These keys are just the ticket. (If you use the keypad keys, be sure the Num Lock feature is off.)

| Move insertion point to | Arrow key | Keypad key |
|---|---|---|
| Beginning of document | Ctrl+Home | Ctrl+7 |
| End of document | Ctrl+End | Ctrl+1 |

## Get Back, Jack!

Sooner or later, you'll start scrolling through a lengthy document, only to discover that you've become lost. Where were you working? Fortunately, Word has a handy "Go Back" command that flips you back to the last three places where you inserted or edited text. To go back, press Shift+F5 (hold down the Shift key and press F5).

**TIP**

As long as you quit Word properly (see Chapter 1), Word remembers the last place you were working when you exited your document. When you reopen a document to work on it more, press Shift+F5. The insertion point magically jumps to the place you left off. For information about opening a document you previously created, see Chapter 5.

# Viewing the Page Layout

Suppose that you print your document, and you (or someone else) marks it up with lots of proposed changes. Your task: Get the document on-screen and make the changes. In this situation, you'll find it really helpful to switch to the Page Layout view. In this view, Word displays your document pages exactly as you see them on the printout. This view is also useful when you are creating page layout elements such as headers and footers (covered in Chapter 11).

To switch to Page Layout view, click open the **V**iew menu and choose **P**age Layout. Word displays the page just like it will look when printed. Unlike Print Preview, this view is fully editable. Page Layout view remains in effect until you change it again.

### Checklist

▼     Take a look at the vertical scroll bar—it has gained two new little buttons on the bottom right. You can click these to move quickly to the same position on the next page or the previous page.

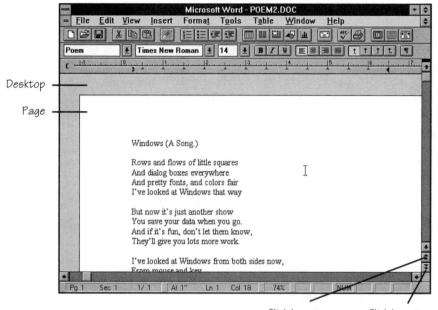

Desktop

Page

Click here to see
the previous page

Click here to see
the next page

"I HATE THIS!"

## The darned text won't fit within the window!

If you have to scroll the screen right and left to deal with long lines of text, click the Zoom Page Width tool (the last tool on the right of the Toolbar). This tool automatically adjusts the size of the window so that the entire line of text fits.

# Displaying Paragraph Marks

When you press Enter, Word places a special, funny-looking character in your document at that exact spot. Only, you don't see it. If you want to

see the paragraph marks, click the paragraph mark button on the far right side of the Ribbon.

Why would you want to display paragraph marks? Well, there's a very good reason indeed. They may be ugly, but you should display those paragraph marks while you're editing. With the little critters visible on-screen, you're less likely to delete one and cause an unwanted paragraph join.

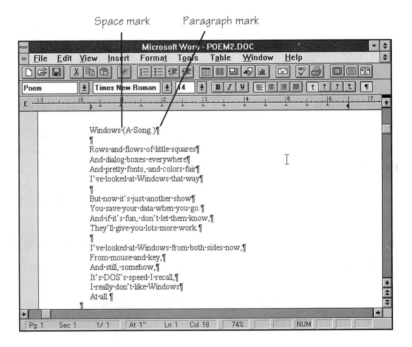

When you display paragraph marks, you also see where you've pressed the Tab key (symbolized by a little right arrow) and the space bar (symbolized by a little dot that floats above the line). You might find it helpful to see these symbols, too, if you're trying to resolve spacing problems. Remember, don't align text with spaces—use tabs instead.

**TIP**

If you've learned touch typing, you probably press the space bar twice after typing a period at the end of a sentence. However, this isn't a good idea with computers. With Word, Windows, fonts, and a decent printer, you possess typesetting technology that would have looked darned good to a professional printer just ten years ago. To give your printouts a professional appearance, leave only one space after each sentence.

# Dash It All

Word has an unusually large number of hyphen options, many of which have names so confusing that even Word gurus can't remember them. Here's a quick guide to these hyphen and dash options, which might prove really useful in a pinch.

**Checklist**

▼ Instead of making a dash with two hyphens, as you do with a typewriter, turn on Num Lock (you see NUM on Word's status bar when Num Lock is on). Then hold down the Alt key and type 0151 on the numeric keypad. Word enters an *em dash* like printers use. An *en* dash is a little shorter and typically is used to separate numbers in a page range. You can enter one of these, too, by pressing the Alt key and typing 0150.

▼ If you're typing a super long word like *antidisestablishmentarianism*, consider that Word might not do a very good job of breaking the line with such a long word. The result might be a big, ugly space,

*continues*

with the long word starting on the next line down. Those who fear such a development would be wise to place an *optional hyphen* within the word—or better yet, two or three of them. An optional hyphen doesn't appear unless Word needs to split the word to make the lines even. To enter an optional hyphen, place the insertion point where you want the hyphen to be placed, and press Ctrl+hyphen.

▼  Hyphenated names are increasingly common these days. What's more, it's considered very poor taste to break them up. Suppose, for example, you're typing a document in which hyphenated names such as Radcliffe-Brown and Evans-Pritchard feature prominently. To prevent Word from breaking the two names, you can use a *nonbreaking hyphen*. This hyphen tells Word, "Don't put a line break here." To enter a nonbreaking hyphen, press Ctrl+Shift+hyphen.

▼  You can also enter a *nonbreaking space*. This keeps Word from breaking up two words that really belong together, like the "6 feet" in "6 feet under." (You don't want the "6" part to appear all by itself at the end of a line.) To enter a nonbreaking space, place the insertion point where you want the nonbreaking space to appear, and press Ctrl+Shift+space bar.

---

**Top Ten Reasons to Use a Typewriter Rather than a Computer**

**10.** A lot cheaper

**9.** No snotty error messages, just that cute little ding

**8.** Real writers don't use computers

**7.** Electricity optional

**6.** Combines keyboard and printer in one compact, space-saving case

**5.** No agonizing decisions over which text typeface (font) to use

**4.** No software needed—load 8 ½ -by-11-inch paper for word processing, index cards for database management, and so on

**3.** Less clutter: no disks, no manuals, no nerds

**2.** You have to learn only a couple of terms, like *platen* and *carriage*

**1.** Tap-tap-tap clatter has promising potential to drive coworkers nuts

# CHAPTER 7

# Searching
# and Replacing

## IN A NUTSHELL

▼ Find text you need to edit

▼ Find a format (bold, italic,
double-spacing)

▼ Replace one word or
phrase with another

▼ Delete a word or
phrase throughout
your document

▼ Replace one format
(bold, for instance)
with another (italic,
for instance)

Let's say you finished that 54-page report late last night. Somewhere, you said something that you sort of regret—something along the lines of, "And if this project isn't implemented immediately, I will submit my resignation." In the cold light of day, this threat now seems intemperate. Out of place. Ill-considered. But where is it?

A sure way to drive yourself batty (not to mention blind) is to try to read a lengthy document on-screen. All those funny, little letters just sort of blend together in the sickly, fluorescent glow. The steady blink of the insertion point begins to hypnotize you. Before long, your eyes cross and you're in a daze. It's far better to let Word do the hunting for you.

With Word's Find command, you can ask Word to hunt through your document, looking for a word or phrase to match. If Word succeeds in finding the text, the program scrolls to the text's location and highlights the text on-screen. You can then nuke it, format it, add to it, or whatever.

With the Replace command, you can search for a word or phrase and replace it with a newer, better word or phrase (for example, you could replace "my resignation" (in "I will submit my resignation") with "a more detailed proposal."

You can even find and replace formats. Suppose, for example, you like to use italics for emphasis, but somewhere you used boldface instead. You want to find the boldface. No sweat! Word can do it. If you like, you can get Word to go through your manuscript and replace all instances of one format with a different format. For example, you can replace bold with italic throughout.

# Finding the Offending Passage
# (The search-and-destroy mission)

When you want to hunt down some text, follow these steps:

**TIP**

> Want to search the whole document? Start by pressing Ctrl+Home to place the insertion point at the beginning of the document.

**1.** Open the Edit menu and choose **Find**. You see the Find dialog box.

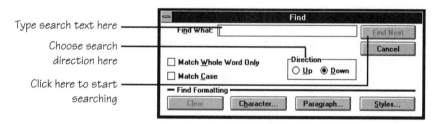

Type search text here

Choose search direction here

Click here to start searching

**2.** In the Find What box, type the word or phrase you want to match. Type carefully, because Word will try to match exactly what you type (except that the program ignores uppercase and lowercase letters).

**3.** Choose **Find Next**.

▼ If Word finds the search word or phrase, you see this text high-lighted on-screen. You can then choose Cancel in the dialog box and edit the text. Or you can choose **Find Next** to find the next matching text.

▼ Did you close the Find dialog box to edit the text? Just press Shift+F4 to continue the search with the same settings. You can then repeat your last action before the search by pressing F4.

▼ You might see a question box with the message `Word has reached the end of the document. Do you want to continue the search at the beginning?` To do so, click **Yes**. To give up the whole idea, click **No**.

▼ What happens if Word can't find the word or phrase? You see an information box telling you that Word has reached the end of the document. Word is being diplomatic here. In a less friendly pro-gram, you would have seen a message like, `Not found`. The Find dialog box is still on-screen, giving you a good opportunity to check the search text for typos.

**EXPERTS ONLY**

## For nitpicky searches

Suppose that you're writing a report for Acme Exterminators, and you want to edit the phrase "Me and Jenkins, we sprayed 1609 Wilton Place last Tuesday." You search for Me, but Word stops at every Acme. To prevent this, you can click the Match **W**hole Word Only check box in the Find dialog box. With this box checked, Word matches the text only if it is preceded and followed by spaces and punctuation.

If you click Match **C**ase, Word searches using the exact pattern of uppercase and lowercase letters you type. If you typed Me, Word would not stop on me, mE, or ME.

If you want to search up from the insertion point, click **U**p in the Direction area.

# Finding a Format (I know I used bold somewhere...)

You can also use Find to find formats. Suppose, for instance, you realize that it wasn't such a good idea, after all, to have boldfaced every occurrence of *me, mine, I,* and *myself* in your annual performance self-evaluation. You think you've fixed all of them, but just to be sure....

To find a format, follow these steps:

**1.** Open the **E**dit menu and choose **F**ind. You see the Find dialog box.

**2.** To search for text that has the format, type the text in the Fi**n**d What box. To search for just the format (in any text), clear all the text (if any) from this text box.

**3.** Do one of the following:

Choose Ch**a**racter to find a character format, such as a font, font size, font style (bold, italic, and so on), underlining, superscript, or subscript. You see the Find Character dialog box. Choose the format you want to find. You can choose more than one format, but this narrows the search to just the passages that have all the formats you choose.

Choose Paragraph to find a paragraph format, such as alignment, indentation, or line spacing options. You see the Paragraph dialog box. Choose the paragraph format you want. As with character formats, you can choose more than one format to find, but this narrows the search to just the passages that have all the formats you choose.

**TIP**

For a rundown on ways to choose options from dialog boxes, see "Your Wish is Word's Command" in the tear-out Mini-Reference at the front of this book.

**4.** When you finish choosing a format (or formats), click OK to get back to the Find dialog box. Next to the word *Format:*, you see the format you want to find (such as *Bold* or *Italic*).

**5.** Choose **F**ind Next. To see what might happen after you start the search, see the checklist titled, helpfully, *Things that might happen after you start the search.*

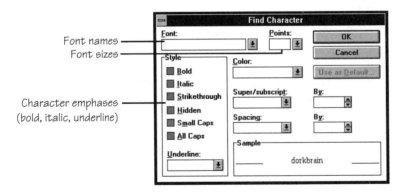

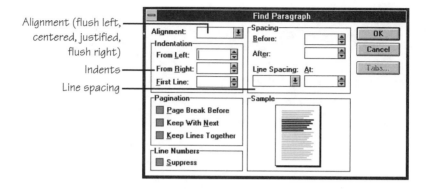

Alignment (flush left, centered, justified, flush right)

Indents

Line spacing

**"I HATE THIS!"**

## When I tried to do a different search, Word couldn't find a thing!

That's because Word remembers the last Find choices you made in this session (since you started Word). If you searched for the Bold format, this setting stays put, even if you close the Find dialog box and reopen it later to perform another search. To clear the format setting, click the Clear button.

# Replacing Text (What I really meant to say was...)

Everything's going fine with your novel. Just peachy. Except, it turns out that there weren't any horses in the Peruvian Andes in the 9th century A.D., the setting you have chosen for your torrid tale of high-altitude romance. You have to go through your whole novel and replace every instance of *horse* with *llama*.

**TIP**

When you replace text, you can replace with confirmation or without. When you replace with confirmation, Word asks your permission before making the replacement. It's a good idea to choose this option at first, so that you can see how Word is making the replacement. If it looks like the replacement is working fine, you can then choose the button that makes the rest of the replacements without confirmation.

Here are the steps to follow for replacing text:

**1.** Open the **E**dit menu and choose Replace. You see the Replace dialog box.

**2.** In the Find What box, type the text you want to search for.

**3.** In the Replace With box, type the text you want Word to insert.

Click here to find the next occurrence

Type the text to search for here

Type the replacement text here

Click here to replace without confirmation

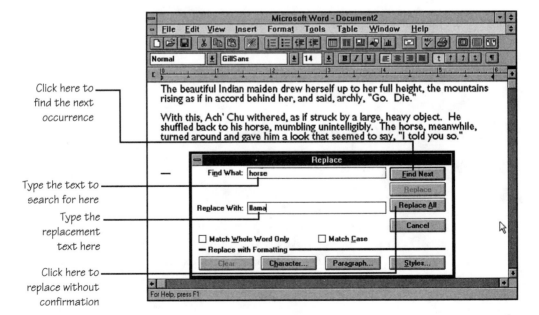

**4.** Choose **F**ind Next. Word searches for the next occurrence of the Find What text and highlights it. You see the highlighted word in the text above the dialog box.

### What to do if Word finds a match

▼ To make the replacement and continue checking with confirmation, click **R**eplace. Word makes the replacement before your eyes, and goes on to the next instance of the search text, if there is one.

▼ To skip this word but keep searching, click **F**ind Next.

▼ To make all the replacements without asking for confirmation, choose Replace **A**ll.

▼ To forget the whole idea, choose Cancel.

The search continues until you reach the end of the document. On the status bar, you find out how many words Word has replaced.

**"I HATE THIS!"**

### It says, "The search text is not found!"

Click OK to get rid of this alert box. The Replace dialog box is still on-screen, which gives you an opportunity to check your spelling for typos. Make the correction, if necessary, in the Find What box. Also, see if the Clear button is dimmed. If it isn't dimmed, then you previously chose to replace a format (as described in the next section), and Word isn't finding your text because the program expects the text to have this format (but it doesn't). Click Clear and try replacing again.

# Replacing with Nothing

Here's a quick way to get rid of an unwanted word or phrase, such as "tubular" or "groovy," that you suspect you've overused. You replace the text with nothing, which deletes the text.

To replace with nothing, follow these steps:

**1.** Open the Edit menu and choose Replace. You see the Replace dialog box.

**2.** In the Find What box, type the text you want to search for. Don't add any extra spaces.

**3.** In the Replace With box, don't type *nothing*. Don't type anything. In fact, delete any text or spaces you see in this box.

**4.** Choose Replace All. Word nukes the word or phrase wherever it occurs, throughout your document. If you're faint of heart, you can choose Find Next and confirm each replacement.

---

**Top Ten Phrases to Delete from Your Novel Unless You Really Want to Reveal That You're Under 34**

**10.** Roller blades/Spandex (tie)

**9.** Cybernated by MTV

**8.** Boomer conspiracy

**7.** Rave party

**6.** Quelle fashion mistake (QFM)

**5.** Sixties envy

**4.** Infotainment

**3.** Gap-clad

**2.** Neon-colored

**1.** Megavitamin smart-drug shake

# Replacing Formats (Getting a makeover)

It seemed like a good idea at the time. Wouldn't it be cute to format every third paragraph with Zapf Chancery italics, just for a change of pace? On the printout, though, it doesn't look so hot. Looks a little out of control, doesn't it? You'd like to change the Zapf Chancery text back to good, old, conservative Times Roman.

To replace one format with another, follow these steps:

**1.** Open the **E**dit menu and choose **R**eplace. You see the Replace dialog box.

**2.** To search for text that has a particular format, type the text in the Find What box. To search for just the format (in any text), clear all the text (if any) from this text box.

**3.** In the Replace With box, type the text you want to replace, if any. If you just want to replace the format, clear all the text (if any) from this text box.

**4.** Place the insertion point in the Find What box and do one of the following:

Choose Character to find a character format, such as a font, font size, font style (bold, italic, and so on), underlining, superscript, or subscript. You see the Find Character dialog box. Choose one of the character formatting options and click OK.

Choose Paragraph to find a paragraph format, such as alignment, indentation, or line spacing options. You see the Paragraph dialog box. Choose one of the paragraph formatting options and click OK.

**5.** Place the insertion point in the Replace With box and do one of the following:

▼ Choose Character to replace the format with a character format, such as a font, font size, font style (bold, italic, and so on), underlining, superscript, or subscript. You see the Find Character dialog box. Choose one of the character formatting options and click OK. (To get rid of a character style format, click the format's check box, which is shaded, to activate it. Then click it again to turn it off.)

▼ Choose Paragraph to replace the format with a paragraph format, such as alignment, indentation, or line spacing options. You see the Paragraph dialog box. Choose one of the formatting options and click OK.

**6.** Choose Find Next. Word searches for the next occurrence of the Find What text and highlights it. You see the highlighted word in the text above the dialog box. For what to do after Word finds a match, see the checklist helpfully titled, "What to do if Word finds a match."

**TIP**

If for some reason the replacement didn't work, there's hope: Click open the **E**dit menu and choose **U**ndo—and do so immediately, before doing anything else such as typing text or choosing a command. Word undoes the replacement.

# CHAPTER 8

# Proofing Text
## (Avoiding Looking Dumb in Print)

## IN A NUTSHELL

- ▼ Check your spelling
- ▼ Find the right word with Thesaurus
- ▼ Find common grammatical and usage errors
- ▼ Hyphenate your document to eliminate "right margin raggedness" (horrors!)

The well-dressed, oh-so-correct document these days commands a lot of attention. That letter-perfect, "in control" look, so perfectly matched with your hip font choices, lets people know that you're not the type to let even the tiniest little error slip through. If you're like me, though, you need help looking your document up and down before showing up in public.

Word's impressive armada of document-proofing tools (Thesaurus, Spelling, Grammar, and Hyphenate) can help you make certain that your document doesn't amount to an embarrassing *faux pas*. This chapter shows you how to use these tools to check your document, but doesn't drown you in details about the six zillion ways you can customize them. Word's document-proofing defaults (the settings chosen at the "factory") are good ones for most users.

**TIP**

Remember that, for all the features discussed in this chapter, you can choose **U**ndo (from the **E**dit menu) to cancel the changes you made—provided you do so immediately after using the feature (Spelling, Thesaurus, Grammar, or Hyphenation). If you perform some other action after using the feature, such as typing some text or using another command, you can't Undo.

# Checking Spelling

People take spelling pretty seriously, as shown by the little *e* that turned the former Vice President of the United States into Mr. Potato(e) Head. It doesn't matter that there are millions of edukated people hoo kant spel, either. Our critics just won't give up.

**"I HATE THIS!"**

## It looked write!

By all means, check your spelling with Word's spelling checker. But don't let Word lull you into a false sense of security. Word can't detect spelling mistakes that involve the use of a correctly spelled word in the wrong place (as Gertrude Stein said of Oakland, California, "Their's no they're there"). I cannot tell you how of ten this occurs. Proof read!

**TIP**

If you want to spell-check just part of a document, select the part first. Then select the Spelling command.

**1.** If you want to spell-check the entire document, press Ctrl+Home to position the insertion point at the beginning of the document.

Word checks from the insertion point forward. If you want to check just part of a document, put the insertion point where you want Word to start checking.

**2.** Open the Tools menu and choose Spelling, or just click the Spelling tool on the Toolbar. Word starts checking your document.

If the program can't find any spelling errors (which is unusual), you see an information box informing you that the spelling check is complete. No praise, no congratulations—just a message that the check is complete. Click OK to continue.

More likely to appear, though, is the Spelling dialog box. Does the appearance of this box mean you've made a spelling error? Not necessarily. Word's spelling checker works by comparing what you've typed to its built-in dictionary, which is pretty huge. Even so, lots of proper nouns

and jargon terms aren't in the dictionary, so Word flags them as potential errors. If the word really is spelled correctly, you can ignore the word or add the word to the dictionary (as explained in the following checklist) so that Word doesn't flag it again.

*This appears when Word finds a spelling boo-boo.*

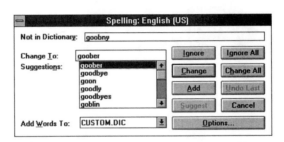

## What to do if Word finds a word that's not in its dictionary

▼ If the word is a correctly spelled proper noun that you plan to use a lot, such as your name, click Add. Word stores this word so that it won't be flagged in later sessions.

▼ If the word is a correctly spelled word that you don't think you'll ever use again, click Ignore (to ignore the word just this once) or Ignore All (to ignore the word for the rest of this document).

▼ If the word really is misspelled, look in the Suggestions list. (If this list is blank, click the Suggest button). If you see the correctly spelled word, just click it to place the word in the Change To box, and click Change. If you want to make the same change throughout your document, click Change All.

▼ To stop the spell check, click the Cancel button.

**"I HATE THIS!"**

## It says, "No suggestions"!

Congratulations! You must have really mangled this word when you typed it. Chances are you transposed some letters, which gives Word fits when it tries to look up suggested words. Try deleting the junk, if any, that's in the Change To box, and type what you think is a close approximation of the word's correct spelling. Then click **S**uggest, and see if the correct spelling appears. If it does, click **C**hange. If it doesn't, try using a more familiar word (which you can insert by typing it in the Change To box and clicking **C**hange).

### Top Ten Clean Words Not Found in Word's Spelling Dictionary

**10.** cyberpunk

**9.** fanzine

**8.** televangelism

**7.** subdirectory (ironic, isn't it?)

**6.** mullah

**5.** lessness

**4.** Maddonnology

**3.** boomer

**2.** jihad

**1.** yuppie

# Using Thesaurus (My word!)

Sometimes, a passage doesn't look right (correct? appropriate?) unless you find the right (fitting? suitable?) word. After all, you wouldn't want your reader to think that you are dull-witted (doltish? dumb?). In such a situation, you might go running for all three pounds of Roget's Thesaurus—but wait! A thesaurus lies above you, hidden on the menu, waiting patiently (calmly? stoically?) for the click of life.

To use Thesaurus, select the word you want to look up, click open the Tools menu, and choose **T**hesaurus. You see the Thesaurus dialog box.

*Tracking down the right word with Thesaurus.*

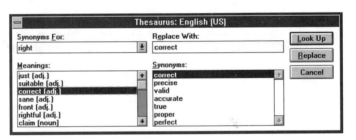

**How to use the Thesaurus dialog box**

▼ In the Synonyms **F**or box, you see the word that Thesaurus is looking up.

▼ In the **M**eanings list, find the word that's closest to the meaning you want, and double-click it. You see the synonyms in the Synonyms list. You may also see new related meanings in the Meanings list. Click one of these, if you like.

▼ If you like one of the words in the Synonyms list, double-click it to place the word in the **R**eplace With box.

▼ After you've maneuvered a word into the **R**eplace With box, you can click Look Up (to see synonyms of this word).

▼ If you want to go back to synonyms you saw previously, click open the Synonyms For list box and choose a previous synonym from the list.

▼ When you've displayed the synonym you want in the Replace With box, click **R**eplace to delete the original word and replace it with this one, or click Cancel to forget the whole idea.

**"I HATE THIS!"**

### There aren't any synonyms for this @#$%$ word!

If all you see is an Alphabetical List rather than a Meanings list, the word isn't in the Thesaurus. If you just misspelled the word, look for the word in the Alphabetical List and double-click it. Alternatively, erase the word in the Replace With box, type the word you want to look up, and click Look Up.

# Checking Grammar (It ain't fun, but it's a good idea)

"These are the voyages of the Starship Enterprise," we are told. In practically the next breath, an infinitive is split: "To boldly go where no one has gone before." You would think that we would put our best foot forward, so to speak, when it comes to first contact with new, exotic alien species (most of which seem to speak English better than we do, anyway, except the Klingons). Those scriptwriters should have used Grammar, which knows how to track down some of those embarrassing grammatical blunders.

**TIP**

Don't take Grammar too literally. For example, it's actually OK to split infinitives when doing so serves the purpose of clarity or emphasis. You may feel cowed by Grammar's schoolmarmish criticism, but remember: You be the judge.

## Doing the Check

Follow these steps to check your document's grammar:

**1.** Place the insertion point where you want to start checking. Word checks forward from this location. If you want to check the whole document, press Ctrl+Home to position the insertion point at the beginning of the document.

**2.** Open the Tools menu and choose **Grammar**. Word starts checking your document.

If the program can't find any grammar errors (which is very unusual), you see an information box giving you readability statistics on your document. This is explained a little later (see "Handy guide for interpreting readability scores"). Click OK to continue.

### What to do if Word finds a grammatical boo-boo

▼ If you don't have the faintest idea what error you've committed, click **E**xplain for a little grammar lesson. To exit the Grammar Explanation window, just double-click the Control menu box in this window.

▼ If the **C**hange button is available, you can click it to have Grammar make the suggested change. This option isn't available very often.

I HATE WORD FOR WINDOWS!

▼ To fix the mistake, you'll probably have to exit the Grammar dialog box and edit your document directly. Just click within your document to activate the document window. The Grammar dialog box stays on-screen. When you've finished making the correction, just click within the Grammar dialog box to re-activate it. Click **Start** to resume checking your document.

▼ To ignore the current error and keep checking the current sentence, click **Ignore**. To skip this sentence and move on to the next, click **Next Sentence**.

▼ To stop Word from nagging you about the current infraction, click Ignore **Rule**.

▼ To cancel this whole, humiliating enterprise and go back to your document, click Cancel and get Mom to correct your document.

## What's It All Mean?

When Word finishes checking your document, you see the Readability Statistics dialog box. This document uses lots of secret, mysterious formulas to determine how much education would be needed to read and understand your document.

**Handy guide for interpreting readability scores**

▼ These days, you shouldn't assume more than about an eighth-grade reading level for most audiences. To reduce the reading level, shorten your sentences. Use simple, familiar words—the good, old Anglo-Saxon ones (like "Fight to the death!") rather than those wordy Latin ones ("Aggression until mortification!").

*continues*

**Handy guide for interpreting readability scores, continued**

▼ A good index to look at is Flesch Reading Ease. 100 means "Very easy," nursery-tale stuff, like "Mary had a rack of lamb" (and a glass of Zinfandel). Anything below 30 is "Very difficult," like "Derrida's conception of ontogenesis is paralleled by his dialectical treatment of transmogrification." (Thanks to that last sentence, this paragraph just barely makes it over the 30 level.)

▼ The last three statistics are supposed to correspond to the grade level of education required to read this stuff, like 5.0 (fifth grade) or 8.4 (eighth grade, plus four months of Miss Turtleby's English class).

▼ Take a look at the Passive Sentences percentage (a passive sentence puts the direct object first, as in "The boo-boo was made by Jane," rather than putting the subject and verb first, as in "Jane made the boo-boo"). By reducing the number of passive voice sentences, you get a much higher readability score.

▼ In case you're curious, these readability indexes employ a mysterious constant (3.82468, the famous Flesch constant).

# Hyphenating Your Document

When you get to the end of a line and Word perceives that the word you're typing won't fit within the margin, the program "wraps" the word down to the next line. If this word happens to be a really big one, such as *antidisestablishmentarianism*, wrapping it down to the next line could leave a really ugly gap. Document design people hate these big gaps because they interfere with the "color" of the page (when you squint, the whole thing is supposed to look like a nice, even gray).

They consider such gaps to be unforgivable *faux pas*, on a par with wearing white socks with black shoes.

You can hyphenate words yourself, if you want. But Word can do it for you—not quite automatically, as you'll see, but close. The program finds places where inserting a hyphen would help to even out line lengths, shows you the place, and even shows you where the program proposes to insert the hyphen. You can approve this, or move the hyphen to another break within the word, or skip hyphenating the word completely.

**TIP**

> Hyphenation is the last thing you should do before printing. Do it only when your document's words are in their final form—after editing, after checking spelling, and after checking grammar. This is because if you make changes after you have hyphenated, some hyphenated words could end up in the middle of lines.

To hyphenate your document, follow these steps:

**1.** Place the insertion point where you want to start hyphenating. If you want to check the entire document, press Ctrl+Home to position the insertion point at the beginning of the document.

**2.** Open the Tools menu and choose **H**yphenate. Word starts checking your document.

If Word can't find any places to hyphenate, you see a message that the hyphenation is complete. That isn't true, really, because Word didn't do anything. Just click OK to return to your document.

If you see the Hyphenation dialog box, Word is showing you where it proposes to insert a hyphen. The black bar shows the proposed hyphen, whereas the faint gray line shows where the right margin lies.

I HATE WORD FOR WINDOWS!

You see this
if Word finds a
place to insert
a hyphen.

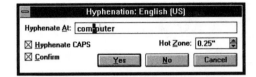

**Hyphenation: English [US]**

Hyphenate At: com|puter

☒ **H**yphenate CAPS          Hot **Z**one: 0.25"

☒ **C**onfirm          [ **Y**es ]   [ **N**o ]   [ Cancel ]

---

### What to do if Word proposes to insert a hyphen

▼   If there are two or more proposed breaks, you can choose the one
you want by clicking it.

▼   To confirm the break, click **Yes**.

▼   To keep Word from hyphenating this word, click **N**o.

▼   To forget the whole thing, click Cancel.

---

If you want to insert hyphens yourself, Chapter 6 will make
you a master of the various hyphens.

**TIP**

# PART III

# Making It Look Nice and Pretty

**Includes:**

# CHAPTER 9

# Making the Characters Look Nice

## (The Costume Department)

## IN A NUTSHELL

▼ Choose more character styles, such as small caps and word underline
▼ Use subscript and superscript
▼ Choose character formats with keyboard shortcuts
▼ Use expanded and condensed text in your document
▼ Change the font
▼ Change the default font and font size
▼ Use symbols
▼ Create cool-looking titles with WordArt

To decide whether your document is "attractive," start by looking with a critical eye at characters. *Characters* refers to the lowest level of formatting in Word—the emphases, fonts, and other things that can happen to letters, numbers, and punctuation marks. With Word, you see these formats right on the screen.

Chapter 3 introduced the essentials of character formatting, including emphases, fonts, and font sizes. This chapter includes additional pearls of character formatting wisdom that might be useful to you.

## More Character Styles

In Word's terminology, character styles include emphases (such as bold, italic, and underline), and some other stuff that you might find useful in your document.

To choose a character format from the Character dialog box, do the following:

**1.** Select the text first. For the lowdown on selection, flip to "Selecting Text" in Chapter 2. Or, just put the insertion point where you want to start typing with the format.

**TIP**

> To display the Character dialog box quickly, double-click the Ribbon (don't double-click a *button* on the Ribbon).

**2.** Open the Format menu and choose **C**haracter. You see the Character dialog box.

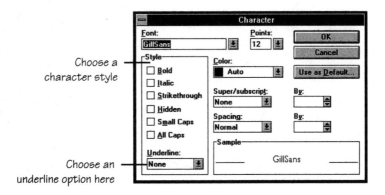

Choose a character style

Choose an underline option here

**3.** Click the style you want.

**4.** Click OK or just press Enter.

### More ways to format characters

▼ ~~Strikethrough~~ is used in legal documents, such as contracts, to indicate which text has been deleted.

▼ Hidden text is useful when you don't want certain text to be printed or displayed. Maybe you want to write a reminder note to yourself. Maybe you want to insert a love message in a memo. You can display hidden text on-screen by opening the Tools menu, choosing Options, and then checking the Hidden Text option in the Options dialog box.

▼ SMALL CAPS look cool for headings and titles. The initial capital letter is full size, but the "lowercase" letters are reduced-size versions of capital letters.

▼ ALL CAPS are just all caps, except this format saves you from having to retype lowercase text so that it appears in all caps.

*continues*

I HATE WORD FOR WINDOWS!

---

**More ways to format characters, continued**

▼ <u>Single Underline</u> is the usual underline option, the one you get if you click the Underline tool on the Toolbar. This option underlines the spaces between words.

▼ <u>Word</u> <u>Underline</u> is also a single underline, except that it doesn't underline the spaces between words.

▼ <u>Double Underline</u> places two lines under the text, leaving no doubt that you really want to call attention to the underlined text, as in "I expect that raise <u>right now</u>."

---

**TIP**

You can choose the **A**ll Caps option in the Character dialog box to capitalize text—but here's a niftier way. To quickly change the case (lowercase and uppercase) of your text without having to retype it, select the text. Then press Shift+F3 several times. As you can see when you try this, this key combination cycles the text through three case patterns: all lowercase letters, all uppercase letters, and the first letter of each word capitalized.

**EXPERTS ONLY**

### Hidden text: Viewing and printing are not the same

If you use hidden text in your document, it won't print. You can print hidden text even if it's not visible, and you can refrain from printing hidden text that is visible. To print hidden text, open the **F**ile menu, choose **P**rint, and then click the **O**ptions button. In the Options dialog box, activate the **H**idden Text option in the Include with Document area, and

then click OK. Click OK again to print your document with hidden text included.

# Keyboard Shortcuts for Character Formatting

If you like the keyboard and don't like the mouse, you're probably not exactly a happy camper in Windows land. But cheer up, bunky. You can use keyboard shortcuts to apply almost all of Word's character formats.

| To apply | Press |
|---|---|
| Bold | Ctrl+B |
| Italic | Ctrl+I |
| Underline (single) | Ctrl+U |
| Underline (word) | Ctrl+W |
| Underline (double) | Ctrl+D |
| Small capital letters | Ctrl+K |
| Subscript (3 points below) | Ctrl+equals sign |
| Superscript (3 points above) | Ctrl+Shift+equals sign |

**"I HATE THIS!"**

## I tried to use the keyboard shortcut, but it put a letter in my document!

To use these keyboard shortcuts, such as Ctrl+B (Bold), you hold down the Ctrl key and then type B (uppercase or lowercase—it doesn't matter which). You shouldn't try to peck both of them at once—it might work, but it might just put an unwanted B into your document. Remember: Hold down the Ctrl key, then peck the letter key.

**TIP**

If you've applied a format and want to get rid of it, you can just select it and use the keyboard shortcut again. For example, if you applied bold but want to remove it, select the boldfaced text and press Ctrl+B. If you applied more than one emphasis (such as bold and italic), you can remove all character formats (including fonts and font sizes) by selecting the text and pressing Ctrl+space bar.

# Using Superscript (E=MC$^2$) and Subscript (H$_2$O)

If you're a genius in fields such as nuclear physics or waste water management, you may need to use superscript and subscript character formats. In superscript, the letters are positioned above the line, whereas in subscript the letters are positioned below the line. By default, Word moves the text up or down 3 points ($\frac{1}{24}$th of an inch), which looks OK—but if you want to get fancy, you can increase or decrease this amount.

To superscript or subscript text, do the following:

1. Select the text first. For the lowdown on selection, flip to "Selecting Text" in Chapter 2.

2. Open the Format menu and choose Character. You see the Character dialog box.

3. Click the drop-down arrow in the Super/subscript box. When the list appears, click Superscript or Subscript. Word puts *3 pt* in the By box.

**4.** If you like, click the up or down arrows (called *spinner controls*) in the By box to change the amount of superscript or subscript. Or just press Tab to highlight the number in the box and type over it.

**5.** Click OK or just press Enter.

**TIP**

> Don't try to enter footnotes manually by using a superscript number and then typing at the bottom of the page. Word can do the whole job automatically, including positioning and numbering the footnotes. For more information, flip to "12 Hot Word Tricks" in the *Quick and Dirty Dozens* section at the end of this book.

# Expanding and Condensing Text

Word's Character dialog box enables you to expand or condense selected text, which has some cool uses. Expanded text looks like this:

e x p a n d e d   t e x t

Condensed text looks like this:

condensed text

Expanded text looks good in titles, whereas compressed text comes in handy when you're trying to squeeze something onto a line.

To expand or condense text, do the following:

**1.** Select the text first. For the lowdown on selection, flip to "Selecting Text" in Chapter 2. Or, just put the insertion point where you want to start typing with the format.

2. Open the Format menu and choose **C**haracter. You see the Character dialog box.

3. Click the drop-down arrow in the Spacing box. When the list appears, click Expanded or Condensed. If you chose Expanded, Word puts *3 pt* in the By box. If you chose Condensed, Word puts *1.75 pt* in this box.

4. If you like, click the up or down arrows (called *spinner controls*) in the By box to change the amount of expansion or condensation. Or just press Tab to highlight the number in the box and type over it. If you're expanding text, you can choose up to 14 points of expansion. If you're condensing text, the maximum is 1.75 points.

5. Click OK or just press Enter.

# Choosing Fonts with the Character Dialog Box

You can choose these formats quickly from the Ribbon, as Chapter 3 stressed, but there's a payoff for choosing them from the Character dialog box: You get to see an on-screen sample of what your characters will look like in your document.

To change the font using the Character dialog box, follow these steps:

1. Select the text that you want to change.

2. Open the Format menu and choose the **C**haracter command.

   You see, once again, the Character dialog box.

3. Click the drop-down arrow in the **F**ont box. When the list appears, click on the font you want.

**4.** If you want to change the font size too, click the drop-down arrow in the **P**oints box and click the size you want.

In the bottom right corner of the dialog box, you see a sample of how the text will look dressed up in this font.

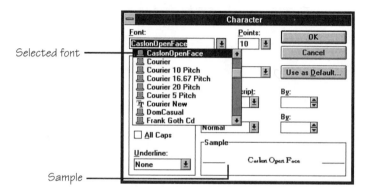

Selected font

Sample

**5.** If you like what you see, click OK. If not, click Cancel to forget about the change.

**EXPERTS
ONLY**

## A handy guide to those funny symbols in the Font list box

In the **F**ont list box (in the Ribbon or Character dialog box), you see little symbols next to the font names. The printer symbol means that the font is a printer font, which will look good when printed, although it might not look good on-screen if you choose a big font size. If you see the TT symbol, the font is a TrueType font. TrueType fonts print well and look good on-screen in all font sizes.

---

**Top Ten Reasons to Use Just Plain Old Courier (the "typewriter" font)**

**10.** Font name easy to choose because it's at the top of the list

**9.** Plain "typewriter" appearance of Courier gives fresh, personalized appearance, as if document were typed for you and you alone on a type-writer

**8.** Courier takes up lots of room, so a four-page college essay assignment looks longer

**7.** All your coworkers are trying to get the boss's attention with these fancy fonts, so your memo will really stand out

**6.** *Real* writers do not concern themselves with the appearance of the text, only its substance

**5.** Courier is a plain-dealing, clean-cut, Ameri-can font, created for American typewriters, and is therefore preferable to fonts like Palatino that are used to print books by con-descending French intellectuals

**4.** Letter typed with Courier font makes it look like you have a secretary, implying that you possess power and status in your organization

**3.** Courier is the default on your computer, and you're too lazy to change it

**2.** Makes a fashion statement—like wearing bag lady fashions

**1.** Great for ransom notes

---

# Changing the Default Font

I can just imagine your morning Word ritual, well entrenched by now. You start Word. You open a new document. You change the font. Why? That bothersome, plain-Jane Courier just won't do for you, no sir. You have fancy plans and you need a fancy font. If you find yourself changing the font or font size every time you start a new document, it's time to start thinking about changing the default font settings.

To change the default font and/or font size, follow these steps:

1. Open the Format menu and choose **Character**. You see the Character dialog box.

2. Choose whatever font or font size options you like.

3. Click the Use as **Default** button. You'll see an alert box asking whether you're really serious about this.

4. Choose **Yes** to confirm your choice, **No** to listen to reason and reject it, or **Help** to make an appointment with a counselor.

5. Later, when you exit Word, say Yes to the prompt `Do you want to save the global glossary and command changes?`.

**TIP**

If you or others can't live with your choice, just repeat these steps to choose a different font or restore the original default font.

# Using Symbols

One great thing about Windows is that you're not stuck with the standard set of 254 characters that limits those poor users of DOS. Packaged with Windows is a Symbols font that includes lots of special symbols for technical, mathematical, and scientific writing. In addition, Windows 3.1 comes with a cool TrueType font called Wingdings, which contains many printer's symbols that you can use for decorative effects in your documents. Every Windows font has lots of additional characters beyond the ones you can access directly from the keyboard, including most of the characters you need for typing passages in the major European languages.

To access these symbols, follow these steps:

**1.** Open the Insert menu and choose Symbol. You see the Symbol dialog box.

**2.** Click the drop-down arrow in the Symbols From list box. Click on the font in which you want Word to draw the symbol. This can be from the Symbol font (technical and scientific symbols), Wingdings (designs including arrows, happy faces, scissors, boxes, dots, and all kinds of stuff), or Normal Text (which gives you access to all the characters included in the font that was current when you chose the Symbol option).

**3.** To choose a character to insert, just double-click it.

Choose a font here

Click one of these symbols

**"I HATE THIS!"**

### I can't get rid of this #@$%# character!

Some special characters are entered in a special environment called a *field*. This protects them from font changes that would change their appearance. However, you can't delete a field by pressing Backspace. If you want to get rid of a character that's in a field, select it and press the Del key.

# Total Font Coolness Department: WordArt

And now for the grand finale in the font sweepstakes: WordArt. This is an accessory program that comes with Microsoft Word for Windows. Basically, WordArt enables you to put neat-looking titles and headings into your document. You can choose from lots of fonts that aren't available in the ordinary Fonts list boxes. What's more, you can make the text go sideways or curve—even into circle, if you like. It's going to ruin your documents for a while, because you won't be able to resist adding huge, garish titles to things like memos requesting another box of paper clips.

To put art created by WordArt into your Word document, follow these steps:

**1.** Open the Insert menu and choose **O**bject. You see the Object dialog box.

**2.** Double-click the MS WordArt option. You see the Microsoft WordArt dialog box.

**3.** In the text box where it says *Your Text Here*, type your text. You see a preview of your text in the Preview box. If you want to start a new line, press Enter.

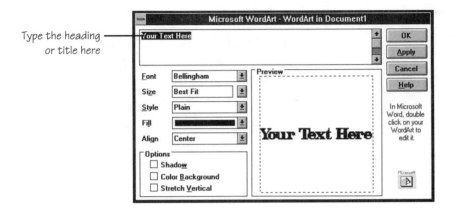

Type the heading or title here

**4.** In the Font list box, choose a font. To see what the fonts look like, choose one and look in the Preview box.

**5.** In the Size box, choose a font size other than Best Fit, unless you're happy with the way the text looks in the Preview box (because that's the size you'll see in your document).

**6.** If you like, choose a style (Upside Down, Arch Up, Arch Down, Button, Slant Up, or Slant Down). To see what these look like, choose one and look in the Preview box.

**7.** Also optional: Choose a text color from the Fill box. The available colors include some grays, which print on most laser or inkjet printers. You can also choose an alignment (the default is centered alignment), shadow text, a colored background, and letters that are stretched, like taffy, along the vertical dimension.

**8.** When you are finished choosing options, click OK or press Enter. If you chose a font size other than Best Fit, you see a dialog box asking whether you want to enlarge the WordArt object in your document. Click OK or press Enter.

Now you see your WordArt title in your document. This one uses the Arch Up style, white text color, and a colored background. The title is positioned in a frame.

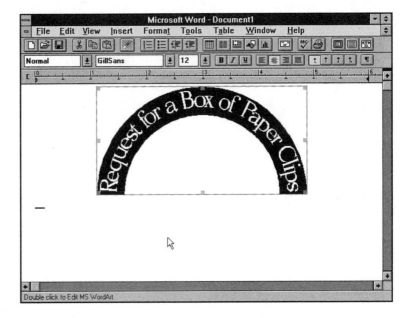

WordArt titles can enliven even the most mundane documents.

**BUZZWORDS**

**FRAME**

A frame is a box that you insert in your document that contains a picture, a drawing, or a WordArt title. When you select the frame, you see the box that surrounds it, as well as the handles (the little, gray squares) you can use to size it (to size the frame, just drag the handles).

**TIP**

Want to edit your WordArt title? Just double-click it. Word starts WordArt and displays your title. Make any changes you like, and click OK until you see your document again. Want to get rid of your WordArt title? Just select it and press the Del key.

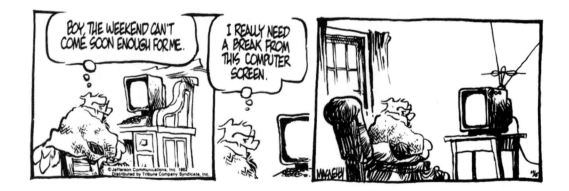

# CHAPTER 10

# Making the Paragraphs Look Nice

## IN A NUTSHELL

- ▼ Indent paragraphs with the Ruler
- ▼ Add blank space between paragraphs
- ▼ Control line spacing
- ▼ Tell Word where (and where not) to start a new page
- ▼ Set custom tabs
- ▼ Add lines, borders, and shading to paragraphs

Chapter 3 introduced essentials of paragraph formatting, including alignments (such as centered and justified), indents, and line spacing. This chapter reveals more ways you can format paragraphs by dragging those little thingies on the Ruler, using the Paragraph dialog box, and performing other amazing tricks. Like the previous chapter, you don't need to read all the way through—you can read just the sections that seem useful or that strike your fancy.

# Indenting Paragraphs with the Ruler

The Ruler is worthy of your attention for a moment here—not because it's particularly thrilling to look at, but because it's a useful way of indenting paragraphs. The trick is learning how to drag all the little black marker things on the Ruler.

**TIP**

If you don't see the Ruler, open the **View** menu and click **Ruler**.

---

**Ruling the Ruler**

▼   The Ruler always shows the indents of the current paragraph—the one in which the insertion point is positioned.

▼   The indent Ruler measures your paragraph from the left margin (not the left edge of the page). So the 0 mark is at the left margin. Word's default page and paragraph formats give you a line length of 6.0 inches.

▼   There are two left indent markers. The top one is the first-line indent marker. This marker controls only the first line of the paragraph. The bottom marker controls the rest of the paragraph.

▼ There is one right indent marker, at the right edge of the Ruler.

▼ To create a first-line indentation for paragraphs, drag the first-line indent marker (the top one on the left).

▼ To indent the entire paragraph, click and drag the bottom left indent marker. Both markers move.

▼ If you want to move the bottom marker independently (and leave the top one where it is), hold down the Shift key as you drag the marker. Holding down the Shift key enables you to move the bottom one independently. A little practice with this pays off.

▼ To indent the paragraph from the right margin, drag the right indent marker.

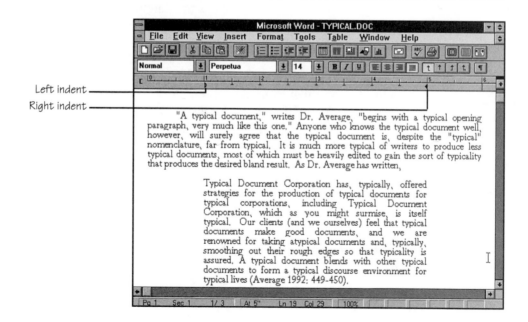

Left indent —
Right indent —

**"I HATE THIS!"**

## I selected more than one paragraph, and the little indent markers dimmed on me!

This is Word's way of telling you that you have selected two or more paragraphs in which the indents differ. You can still move the markers, though. If you do, the changes you make apply to all the selected paragraphs.

# Setting Tabs

Back in the old days of clunky typewriters, you set a tab by physically moving the tab stop. When you pressed Tab, the whole carriage zoomed over to the stop in a thrilling, table-shaking lurch. Setting tabs with Word isn't quite as dramatic. But on the positive side, it's much easier—you can do so just by clicking their locations on the Ruler.

By default, Word gives you tabs every half-inch across the page. These are shown on the Ruler by miniature, upside down *T*s that hang like little bats under the half-inch marks. If you want, you can set custom tabs. When you set a custom tab, Word deletes any of the default tabs to the left of the custom tab.

The basic thing to remember about custom tabs is that your tab stop choices apply to the selected paragraphs, not the whole document. On the Ruler, you see the tab stops that have been set (if any) for the currently selected paragraph. Because you can set different tab stops for each paragraph, you can have as many different custom tab layouts as you have different paragraphs.

# Tab Types

Word's tabs are a bit more complicated than a typewriter's in that you can choose four different kinds.

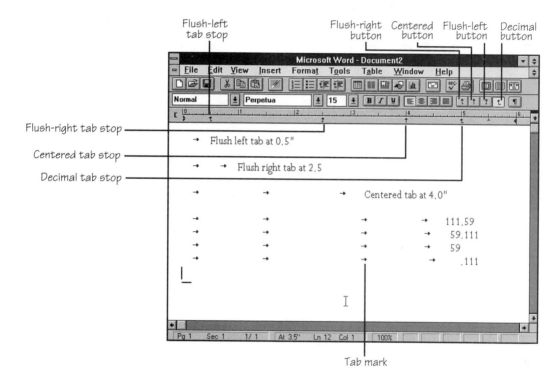

Flush-left tab stop

Flush-right button  Centered button  Flush-left button  Decimal button

Flush-right tab stop

Centered tab stop

Decimal tab stop

Flush left tab at 0.5"

Flush right tab at 2.5

Centered tab at 4.0"

111.59
59.111
59
.111

Tab mark

**Tab-setting options**

▼ A flush-left tab stop aligns the text flush left, beginning where the tab is set.

▼ A centered tab stop centers the text at the tab stop. This isn't necessarily centered on the page—it all depends on where you set the tab stop.

*continues*

135

▼ A flush-right tab stop aligns the text flush right, with the end of the text appearing where the tab is set.

▼ A decimal tab stop aligns at the decimal point, and is usually used for numbers. This is obviously a very cool thing for typing up a column of numbers, or when you want a numbered list to line up correctly even when you use double digits.

## Stop! Tab!

To set a tab stop, follow these steps:

**1.** Position the cursor in the paragraph or select the paragraphs that you want to format with custom tab stops, or press Enter to start a new paragraph that will have the custom tabs.

**2.** On the Ribbon, click the tab button you want.

**3.** On the Ruler, but on the lower half of the measuring stick, click where you want the tab to be set. You see little arrows. Their shape tells you which kind of tab you've set.

**4.** If you need to adjust the tab's position, just click the tab arrow on the Ruler and drag it left or right.

**TIP**

To delete a tab stop, just click and drag the little arrow down and off the Ruler.

After you have set tabs, you press the Tab key to advance the insertion point to the next tab stop, just as you do with a typewriter.

**TIP**

Take my advice—don't use custom tabs to type a fancy table, one of those jobs with box headers and lists of numbers. By far the easiest way to do this is to create a table, which is the subject of Chapter 14.

## More Fun with Paragraphs

The Paragraph dialog box enables you to choose all the paragraph formats Word offers, including many options that are easier to choose in other ways (such as alignments and indents). But there are a few things that you can only do with the Paragraph dialog box, as discussed in this section. To view the Paragraph dialog box, open the Format menu and choose **P**aragraph.

The Paragraph dialog box, with its six zillion options, most of which you can safely ignore.

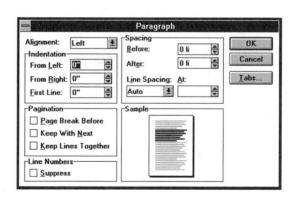

**TIP**

A fast, mousy way to open the Paragraph dialog box is to double-click the top half of the Ruler. Double-clicking the bottom half opens the Tab dialog box.

**"I HATE THIS!"**

### Do I really have to learn all six zillion of these paragraph formatting options?

No. To align paragraphs, just click the alignment buttons on the Ribbon. You can indent from the left by clicking the Nest Paragraph tool. You can add a blank line before the paragraph by pressing Ctrl+O (the letter, not the number). You can change between single and double line spacing with Ctrl+1 and Ctrl+2. The only time you need the Paragraph dialog box is if you want to use one of the formats that isn't available in easier ways. The following sections indicate some useful stuff that you find in this dialog box, but I skip a lot of stuff because there are easier ways of doing it.

## Adding Lots of Space under a Heading

The easiest way to add blank lines is to use the Ctrl+O shortcut. This adds one blank line before a paragraph. If you want to add blank lines after a paragraph, such as a document title, you can use the Paragraph dialog box. In the Spacing area, locate the After box. By default, this says *0 li* (*li* is short for *line*). Click the little up arrow thingie (this is called a spinner ) until you have set the spacing the way you want. If the number is too high, click the down arrow. Notice the Sample diagram to show the chosen spacing. Click OK or press Enter to confirm your choice.

**TIP**

Remember, if you've added blank lines before or after a paragraph, Word copies this format to the next new paragraph you create when you press Enter. You can start a new line without any blank spacing by pressing Shift+Enter (the New Line command).

**"I HATE THIS!"**

### C'mon. Why can't I just press Enter to create blank lines?

Well, you can. Everyone does. I do. There's no real harm in it. But, there's a good reason to add blank lines with the Spacing options (and Ctrl+0). Suppose you type a single-spaced document, but you create a blank line between each paragraph by pressing Enter. Then you decide to double-space your document. After you do, you get an ugly space of four blank lines between each paragraph, because Word double-spaced the blank line as well as the text paragraphs. You'll have to go through your whole document and delete all the blank lines manually, which is kind of a drag. If you had added the blank lines with Ctrl+0 (the letter), you could remove them by selecting the whole document and pressing Ctrl+0 (zero).

**EXPERTS ONLY**

### Read this only if you're curious about Word's measurement options

By default (at least in the U.S.), Word for Windows uses inches as the unit of measurement. If you type a measurement number such as 1.2, Word assumes you mean 1.2 inches.

*continues*

**139**

## Read this only if you're curious about Word's measurement options, continued

An exception: In the Paragraph dialog box, vertical spacing measurements (such as **B**efore and Aft**e**r) are measured in lines (li). If you'd like to go metric, you can change the default unit of measurement to centimeters (2.54 centimeters equal 1 inch). If you're a print-shop type or wannabe desktop publisher, you can choose points (72 points equal 1 inch) or picas (12 picas equal 1 inch).

To choose the default unit of measurement, open the T**o**ols menu, choose **O**ptions, and click the General icon. Then drop down the **M**easurement Units box and click the measurement unit you want. Close the Options dialog box by clicking OK.

## Controlling Page Breaks

In the Pagination area of the Paragraph dialog box are three options that are great for controlling page breaks. As explained in Chapter 4, using these options gives you better control over page breaks.

### Controlling page breaks with the Pagination options (Paragraph dialog box)

▼ To tell Word to always break a page before the current paragraph (the one in which the insertion point is positioned), check the Page Break Before option. This is great for chapter titles in a novel or thesis, or any other heading where you want the heading to appear on a new page.

▼ To tell Word to keep the current paragraph with the text that follows, check the Keep with **N**ext option. This is great for making sure that a heading or subheading doesn't get left all by its lonesome at the bottom of a page (but see the Tip that follows).

▼ To tell Word to never, never place a page break within the lines of a paragraph, check the **K**eep Lines Together option. This is great to keep a quote or poem together on a page. (Poets, remember, if you break lines with the New Line command, Word regards the result as a single paragraph, so the poem will be kept together with this option. If the entire poem doesn't fit, it's pulled to the next page.)

**TIP**

Here's yet another good reason for not entering blank lines by pressing Enter. Suppose you type a heading, and then you press Enter to make a blank line under it. In Print Preview, you see that Word has positioned the heading at the bottom of the page (Murphy's Law, remember?). So you format the heading with the Keep With Next option. You look at Print Preview again, but Egad! It didn't work!

Here's why. When you choose the Keep with Next option, you tell Word to keep the paragraph with the next paragraph. Well, as far as Word is concerned, a blank line is a paragraph. OK, I know, this is stupid and maddening. To cure the problem, though, you need only remember to enter blank lines with Ctrl+O (or the Spacing options in the Paragraph dialog box). A blank line entered this way is not a paragraph. So, when you use the Keep with Next option, Word keeps the heading with the following text.

# Adding Borders and Shading

Does your document look too typical? You can jazz it up with lines, borders, and shading. Like tabs, these formats also are attached to specific paragraphs, which means you can vary them paragraph by paragraph. In the following figure, you see a bold, thick line under the first paragraph (the document title), whereas the paragraph to follow—the corporation's name and address—is boxed with a double line and shaded with a rich, deep color.

A typical document jazzed up with lines, borders, and shading.

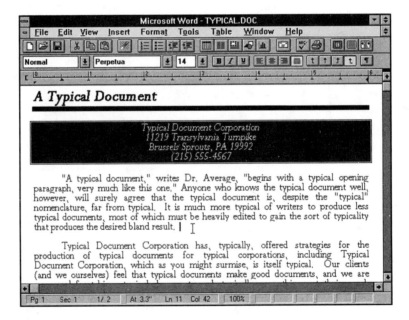

**TIP**

You can add borders to a graphic, too, such as a picture or one of those nifty WordArt titles discussed in Chapter 9. Just select the graphic and follow the steps given here.

To add borders and shading to a paragraph (or paragraphs) in your document:

**1.** Select the paragraph or paragraphs to which you want to add lines, borders, and shading.

**2.** Open the Format menu and choose **B**order. You see the Border Paragraphs dialog box.

**3.** Do one of the following:

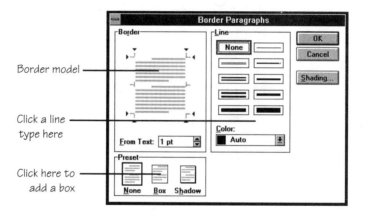

Border model ⟶

Click a line type here ⟶

Click here to add a box ⟶

▼ If you just want to add a box to the selection, click a line type other than None, and click **B**ox or Shadow.

▼ To add just one line above, below, to the left, or to the right of the paragraph, do this: In the Border area, click where you want the line to appear. The funny triangle thingies indicate which border is selected. Then, click a line type other than None.

▼ If you want to add two or three borders, do this: In the Border area, hold down the Shift key and click all the places where

you want borders. If you click too many borders, you can re-move one by clicking it again with the Shift key held down. Then, click a line type other than **None**.

**4.** If you want to add shading, click the Shading button. You see the Shading dialog box.

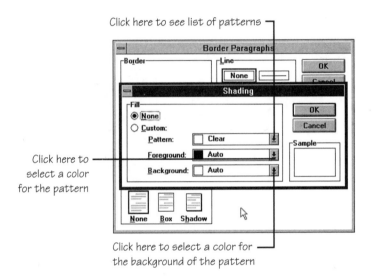

Click here to see list of patterns ⌐

Click here to
select a color
for the pattern

Click here to select a color for ──
the background of the pattern

**5.** Do one or more of the following:

▼ In the **Pattern** list box, choose a shading pattern. This is the place to add shadings for black and white printers. The shad-ings are expressed in percentages, with 5% being really light and 90% being really dark. You can also choose from lots of crosshatching patterns, which have cute names like "grid" and "trellis."

▼ In the **Foreground** list box, you can choose a color, if you have a color printer, or gray shades for black and white printers. Your color choice affects the dots or lines used to make the shading or pattern.

▼ In the **B**ackground list box, choose the color or gray shade you want Word to use in back of the dots or lines that make up the shading pattern.

**6.** Click OK or press Enter. You see the Borders dialog box again.

**7.** Click OK or press Enter to return to your document and see your border and shading choice.

**TIP**

Word always makes the borders go with the current indent settings. To get a nice, compact box like the one shown in the following figure, indent the paragraph from both sides by dragging the indent thingies on the Ruler.

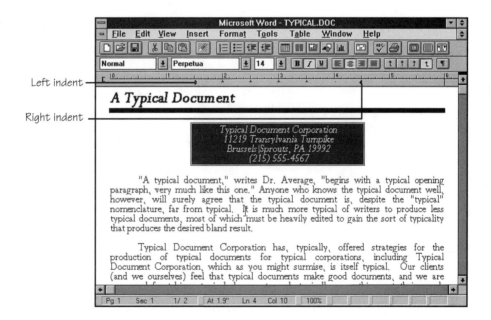

**Top Ten Ways U.S. History Would Have Differed Had Word Processing Been Available in the U.S. Since 1750**

**10.** Declaration of Independence would look more impressive with cool Zapf Chancery italic font; could have been faxed directly to King George

**9.** Mischievous soldiers use the on-line thesaurus to come up with new, derisive nicknames for "Stonewall" Jackson

**8.** Many additional civil liberties granted because it would have been so easy to insert amendments when typing up the Bill of Rights

**7.** Paul Revere could have sent famous "one if by land, two if by sea" message via electronic mail instead of running that poor horse so hard

**6.** George Washington would have said, "I cannot tell a lie. I deleted the document about the cherry tree"

**5.** MacArthur could have concealed activities, and never have gotten fired by Truman, by burying reports of Korean War activities in incomprehensible 500-page documents

**4.** Hundreds of 1929 businessmen are spared when they decide to exit Windows rather than windows

**3.** Morale at Valley Forge higher because of snazzy newsletter George put together

**2.** Francis Scott Key uses laptop to compose the National Anthem; correctly spells "over."

**1.** Glitch in spell-checker causes confusion for Union soldiers, who think they are going to fight the "Battle of Chipmunk" rather than the Battle of Chickamaugua

# CHAPTER 11

# Making Pages Look Nice

## IN A NUTSHELL

- ▼ Set left and right margins
- ▼ Set top and bottom margins
- ▼ Add headers and footers
- ▼ Create a newsletter with two columns

Word has three different formatting zones, which are quaintly referred to as *domains*: the character, the paragraph, and the page. This chapter examines page formats, which have to do with matters such as margins, page breaks, columns, headers, and footers. In the well-established tradition of this book, it steadfastly ignores advanced or seldom-used features that most Word users never use, such as printing with a Czechoslovakian paper size or using the auxiliary paper tray of a $12,000 printer. What's in this chapter is the bottom-line, "you're sure to do this" stuff that makes the *I Hate...* series famous.

# Setting Margins (The definitive act of page design)

By default, your Word documents have 1-inch margins at the top and bottom, and 1.25-inch margins on the left and right. These margins are fine for short documents such as letters and memos; however, if you're writing a lengthy document such as a report, a novel, or romantic memoirs, you may want to change the margins to 1 inch all around (or some other setting).

**TIP**

Remember the difference between margins and indents. If you just need to indent one or a few paragraphs, don't change the margins to do this. Indent the *paragraphs*, as described in Chapter 10. You should change the margins only when you want the change to affect the whole document.

# Changing the Left and Right Margins

The easiest way to change the left and right margins is to use the Ruler. At the left of the ruler is a little bracket, which is actually a clickable thing. It's called the Scale icon. If you click the Scale icon, the ruler changes. It has two brackets, a left one and a right one.

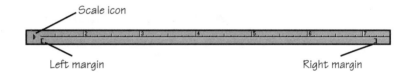

Scale icon

Left margin           Right margin

**Changing left and right margins with the Ruler**

▼ The Ruler now measures the whole page. The left margin bracket is set at the 1.25-inch mark, whereas the right margin bracket is set at the 7.25-inch mark. (Word uses 1.25-inch margins on the left and right, by default).

▼ To change a margin setting, drag the bracket left or right.

▼ Your change affects the whole document, not just the current paragraph or page.

▼ To see the indent Ruler again, just click the indent marker icon at the left of the Ruler.

# Changing Top and Bottom Margins

If you want to change the top and bottom margins, you have to use the Page Setup command—there's no way to do this with the Ruler (although you might try pressing down hard on the top of the monitor).

**CHAPTER 11**

Open the Format menu. Then choose the Page Setup command. You see the Page Setup dialog box. You can use this dialog box to do lots of things that this chapter doesn't go into, such as changing the default paper size and telling expensive printers which paper tray to use. Here, the concern is with the Margins options, which are displayed by default when this dialog box pops on-screen.

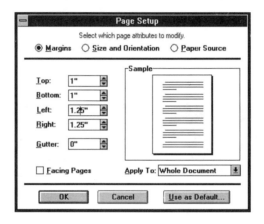

*Use the Page Setup dialog box to change the top and bottom margins.*

You can change the top and bottom margins, as well as the left and right margins, with this dialog box. What's cool about this dialog box is the Sample box, which shows what your margins are going to look like.

To change the margins, you change the number in the box by using the spinner controls. (If you prefer, you can type the number directly. You don't have to type the inches symbol, because that's Word's default measurement format.) When you finish setting the margins, choose OK.

---

**More margin-setting facts**

▼  Would you like to change the default margins for all the documents you create? Click the Use as Default button. When the question box appears, click **Yes**.

▼ If you're planning to duplicate your document using both sides of the page, click the Facing Pages option. The Sample box changes to show two pages. If you added a gutter, you see the gutter on the right side of the left page, and the left side of the right page—which is cool, because that's where you're going to bind the pages together.

▼ The Gutter setting lets you add space for stapling or binding the pages together along the left side of the page. If you add a gutter of 0.5 inches, Word adds that amount to the left margin. (The gutter is shown with dark shading.)

▼ If you really want to change margin settings in the midst of your document, place the insertion point where you want the change to occur, click open the Format menu, and choose Page Setup. Choose the new margin settings you want, and choose This Point Forward from the Apply To list box. Click OK or press Enter to confirm your change. The change takes effect on the current page and through the remaining document.

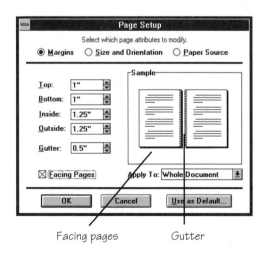

Facing pages          Gutter

**"I HATE THIS!"**

### It cut off part of my text!

Most laser and inkjet printers cannot print within a half-inch or so of the edge of the page; they need this area to grab and hold the page while printing the text. If you tried to use really narrow margins (like 0.35 inch) and some of the text got cut off, it's not Word's fault. And it's not my fault, either. It's the printer's fault. So don't blame us. Just calm down and use thicker margins.

## Adding Headers and Footers

Headers and footers are short titles or other text that prints within the top (header) or bottom (footer) margin of each page of your document. Headers and footers are often used to remind the reader of the document or chapter's title or the author's name. They may also include page numbers. Company reports might also include the date and time.

You can add headers or footers (or both) to your Word document, and it's a great idea. For example, you can add a header on the second page of a letter that indicates the date, the page number, and the correspondent's name. For a lengthy document, you can add a header or footer that includes the document's title and the page number.

**TIP**

If you create headers or footers, don't use the Page Numbers option (Insert menu) to add page numbers. Add them with the Header or Footer window instead, as described in the following steps.

It's easy to add a header or footer. Just follow these steps:

**1.** Make sure you are viewing your document in Normal view. If you are viewing your document in Page Layout view, click open the **View** menu and choose **Normal**.

**2.** From the View menu, choose **Header/Footer**. You see the Header/Footer dialog box. This dialog box contains the current settings for header and footer locations within the margin. These settings should be OK.

*The Header/ Footer dialog box.*

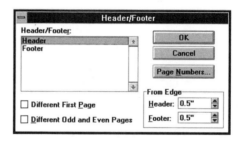

**3.** Because you probably don't want your header or footer to print on the first page, click the Different First Page option. After you click this option, you see First Header and First Footer in the Header/Footer list box. You can use these options later, if you really want to put a header or footer on the first page.

**4.** In the Header/Footer list, select Header or Footer. If you clicked the Facing Pages option in the Page Setup dialog box, you see options for Even Header, Even Footer, Odd Header, and Odd Footer. You can make different headers and footers for odd and even pages. You have to do this procedure twice (or four times, if you want both headers and footers), so just choose one to get started. Have fun.

**5.** Click OK or press Enter. You see the Header or Footer pane, which opens on the bottom half of your screen.

**6.** Type the header or footer text, such as a document or chapter title. To add the page number, date, or time, just click the appropriate button. The header or footer is already set up with a centered tab in the middle and a flush-right tab on the right.

Note that you just can't type the page number—to get the correct page numbers in your document, you have to click the little # button so that Word enters a funny, hidden thing that automatically shows the number of the current page.

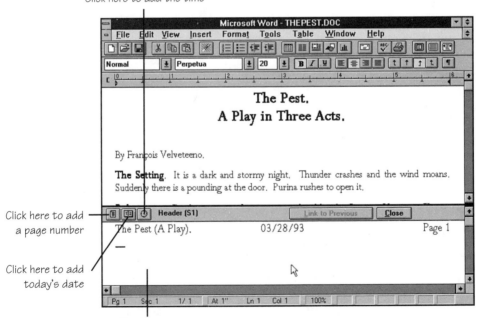

Click here to add the time

Click here to add a page number

Click here to add today's date

Header pane

**7.** To confirm your header or footer and close the pane, click Close.

After you create the header or footer, you don't see it in Normal view. To view the header or footer, switch to the Page Layout view or use Print Preview.

Header

Print Preview of document with a header.

**"I HATE THIS!"**

## My header has the wrong font!

Word doesn't automatically give your header or footer the same font that your document has. If the font is different, edit the header or footer text (as described in the following Tip) and change the font.

**TIP**

If you want to edit the header or footer you have created, no problem. Just repeat these steps. When the header or footer dialog box appears, you see the header or footer text you created. Make any change you want.

# Using Columns (News Flash! News Flash!)

People publish newsletters on every conceivable subject. On the smallest scale, you find the brag letters sent around on holidays ("John was promoted to Vice President and Kathie won the concerto competition, but on the down side, the dog died"). Moving up, organizations of all kinds publish newsletters with larger circulations—newsletters that, before the advent of word processing technology, would have looked like they had been pathetically pecked out on cheap typewriters. With the aid of today's fonts, graphics, and laser printers, not to mention programs like Word, a newsletter that looked like an amateur typed product yesterday can look like an amateur desktop published product today.

You might not believe it from looking at the figure, but creating a newsletter like this is really easy. It's a matter of using a section break and two-column formatting—it's all stuff you can do.

**TIP**

If you just want to set up columns—you don't want the banner stuff—just follow steps 9 and 10.

A newsletter created with Word and WordArt (before running the spelling checker).

To set up a newsletter, follow this ten-step program:

**1.** Get your favorite soft drink. I recommend Mountain Dew. Twice the caffeine. If you want to send a message your readers will never forget, try Jolt Cola.

**2.** Open a new Word document.

**3.** Important: Press Enter three or four times so that you have some paragraphs to work with. If you can't see the paragraph symbols, click the Paragraph mark display button on the Toolbar.

**4.** Put the insertion point in the first paragraph (before the first paragraph mark). Click open the Insert menu and choose Object. From the Object list, choose WordArt. Prepare a title in WordArt, and choose OK to add the title to your newsletter. (For the lowdown on WordArt, flip to Chapter 9.)

**5.** Put the insertion point in the second paragraph and type a banner heading (like the one that says "International Association of Hamster Fanatics"). To type the date flush to the right margin, set a flush-right tab right smack on the right margin mark. (For the lowdown on tabs, flip to Chapter 10.)

**6.** With the insertion point still in the second paragraph, open the Format menu and choose **B**orders. Add borders to the top and the bottom of the paragraph to give that cool, "newspaper" look to the banner. (For more information on adding borders, flip to Chapter 10.)

**7.** Is the insertion point still in the second paragraph? Good. Click open the Format menu again, choose **P**aragraph, and add a couple of blank lines after the banner.

**8.** Put the insertion point in the third paragraph. From the **I**nsert menu, choose **B**reak. You see the Break dialog box. In the Section Break area, choose Continuous. After you click OK, you see a section break in your document. It looks like a double row of dots across your screen.

**BUZZWORDS**

**SECTION and SECTION BREAK**

You can divide a Word document into two or more sections, each of which can have its own page and footnote numbering sequence, as well as its own headers and footers (text printed within the margins). This feature was included for unfortunate souls such as myself who must write lengthy documents broken down into chapters. By putting each chapter into its own section, you can do fancy stuff like grouping all the footnotes to print at the end of the section. A section break is a double row of dots across the screen that shows where you've inserted the section break (you do this with the Break dialog box).

**9.** With the insertion point still in the third paragraph (below the section break), click down on the Columns tool on the Toolbar. You see a box with four text columns. Drag over the first two until you see *2 Columns* at the bottom of this box. Then release the mouse button. This gives the two-column format.

*Choosing a two-column format.*

**10.** Type the text. If you want to start a new column before getting to the bottom of the page, click open the Insert menu, choose **B**reak, and choose Column Break in the Insert area. Click OK to confirm the break.

*"I HATE THIS!"*

### It's only letting me type in the left column!

Take it easy—it only looks that way because you're working in Normal view. In Normal view, you just see one long column on the left. To see what your newsletter is really going to look like, click open the **V**iew menu and choose **P**age Layout. Now your document looks more like the one in the figure, with two columns visible on-screen. (You have to type enough text to get to the second column, though.)

**Top Ten Least Popular Amateur Newsletters**

**10.** Gilligan's Island Fan Club

**9.** Raising Toads for Fun and Profit

*continues*

**CHAPTER 11**

I HATE WORD FOR WINDOWS!

**Top Ten Least Popular Amateur Newsletters, continued**

**8.** Charles Manson Collectibles Digest

**7.** Psychotic Loners' Journal of Violent Revenge Fantasies

**6.** UFO Abduction Victims' Recovery Hotline

**5.** Monthly Review of All The Bad Things That Just Might Happen

**4.** Tips and Tricks for Household Dust Mite Eradication

**3.** Monthly Airline Maintenance Infraction Update for Nervous Fliers

**2.** Risky Investments that Have Lost Big Money in the Past, But Who Knows?

**1.** Let's Share Road Kill Recipes

# PART IV

# Cool Things

**Includes:**

# CHAPTER 12

# Crank Out Letters and Faxes Fast

## IN A NUTSHELL

▼ Store your name and address so that Word can add it to your letters automatically

▼ Store your correspondents' names and addresses so that you don't have to retype them

▼ Create and print envelopes quickly

▼ Create a fax cover fast

I HATE WORD FOR WINDOWS!

t's frustrating. We computer book authors try our darndest, but people still insist on buying $5,000 worth of computer and using it like $200 worth of typewriter. Frankly, computers are just so much junk unless they can save you time, effort, and energy. The worst thing about personal computers is that they don't do this automatically. Computers are notorious for adapting to our old-fashioned work habits.

Some of the best computer time-savers require that you do things a little differently than you would with a typewriter. This means a few new concepts and terms, but the payoff is worth the price of admission. The stuff in this chapter is guaranteed to save you lots of time and computer hassle. It focuses on one of the things you'll do most often with your computer—crank out letters, complete with nicely printed envelopes and fax cover letters, to which Word adds names and addresses automatically.

# Using Word's Letter Templates (Be clever, work less)

Answered those letters lately? Written to Mom? OK, it's a hassle. But consider this: How would you like Word to store your return address and add it automatically to letters you write? To add today's date to your letters automatically? To store your correspondent's name and address automatically, so that when you write to the same address in the future, you can just choose it from a stored list? To add a header on the second and subsequent pages that includes your correspondent's name, the date, and the page number? To enter your name automatically in the Publisher's Clearinghouse Sweepstakes?

You are probably thinking, "This cannot be." But it's true, and what's more, it's easy. In this section, you learn how to use Word's supplied document templates, which come with their own macros, to crank out letters super-quick.

**BUZZWORDS**

**TEMPLATE**

A "generic" version of a document that includes just the stuff you need to start the document. This includes fonts, formats, and other things that help you avoid duplicating work every time you start a new document of this type. When you open a template, it goes into an untitled document that you can save with a different file name. This preserves the original template unaltered.

**BUZZWORDS**

**MACRO**

A series of Word commands that are stored and can be "played back" when you like. Some of the templates supplied with Word have macros that run automatically.

## Standard Letter Templates

Word comes with four standard letter templates that are based on a widely used secretarial handbook. Table 12.1 summarizes these templates.

| Table 12.1. Word's Letter Templates | |
|---|---|
| Template | What it does |
| LETBLOCK | This creates a standard block letter format, with everything formatted flush left. |
| LETMODBK | This creates a modified block letter format, with the closing stuff ("Sincerely yours…") indented about four inches. |
| LETMDSEM | This creates a modified semi-block letter, with the closing stuff indented. Also, each paragraph in the letter is indented. |
| LETPERSN | This creates a modified block letter like LETMODBK does, but it doesn't include all the fancy stuff such as your title or the notations after the closing (such as who gets carbon copies). |

# Opening a Template for the First Time

When you open a letter template for the first time, the program prompts you to supply extensive information about yourself (such as your name, your address, your telephone and fax number, and your astrological sign) and the person you're writing to. This process is a little time-consuming. Yes, it's 15 long steps. But you have to fill in the information only once.

The next time you want to write a letter, the program automatically puts in your return address. You can type a new correspondent's name and address, if you want, or choose an existing one from a list.

To open a letter template for the first time, follow these steps:

**1.** From the **F**ile menu, choose **N**ew. You see the New dialog box.

**2.** In the **U**se Template list, choose one of the first four options—LETBLOCK, LETMDSEM, LETMODBK, or LETPERSN, and click OK. You see a dialog box informing you that this is the first time you have used this template, and that it will take a little while to prepare it.

**3.** Click OK or press Enter to continue. You see another dialog box telling you to enter your sender information in the next dialog box.

**4.** Click OK or press Enter to continue. You see the Enter Sender Information dialog box. There's a lot to fill out, but you only do this once.

**5.** Choose a title like Mr. or Ms.

**6.** Click in the first text box to activate it, and type the requested information. To get to the next text box, you can click it or just press Tab—but don't press Enter.

**7.** Repeat this step until you have filled out all of the text boxes. You can skip the **W**riter's Initials or **T**ypist's initials, though, if you're planning to type your own letters. Fill these out if you're typing someone else's letters.

**Enter Sender Information:**

Enter YOUR name and address. It is used in letters and envelopes you create. You only need to do this once.

Choose a title here ——— Mr.    F̲ull Name:
                         Mr.
                         Ms.    S̲uffix:
                         Miss

Click in the box to type the    P̲osition:
required information            Co̲mpany:
                               Address 1̲:
Leave this blank if it's not needed ——— Address 2̲:
                               C̲ity:
                               S̲tate:         Z̲ip Code:

                               Phone N̲umber:              OK
                               Fa̲x Number:              Cancel
                               W̲riter's Initials:
                               T̲ypist's Initials:

Skip these if you type your own letters

**8.** Click OK or press Enter to confirm filling out your information. You see a dialog box asking you whether the information is correct.

**9.** Read the sender information carefully. If it's correct, click **Confirm**. If it's not correct, click **Edit**, which brings back the Enter Sender Information box. After you correct the information, click OK and then click **Confirm**. You next see the Letterhead Options dialog box.

**10.** Do one of the following:

▼   If you're going to use your printed company letterhead paper, just click OK or press Enter. With this option, Word skips printing your name and return address at the top of the first page.

▼    If you're going to use blank paper and want to print your own letterhead, activate the **B**lank Paper option and click OK. With this option, Word prints your name and return address at the top of the first page. You'll see a dialog box that shows you what Word proposes to place at the top of the first page; if this is OK, click OK. If not, click Edit, and type the information you want to include. Be sure to click Shift+Enter at the end of each new line rather than Enter. When you're done, click OK.

**11.** The next dialog box asks you how you want the header aligned. You can choose an alignment option other than the default— centered is a good choice. Click OK to continue.

**12.** Sit tight, because all kinds of weird, automatic things happen for a while. Finally, you see a dialog box informing you that you can change the options you've chosen with Set Letter Options (Forma**t** menu). This option is available only when one of the letter templates is open. Click OK to continue.

**13.** You see the Letter Addresser dialog box. Because this is the first time you have used this feature, you will add a new address. So choose **N**ew.

**14.** You see the Address the letter to: dialog box. This looks just like the sender information box, except you type your correspondent's information here. You need to fill out the name, address, city, and ZIP, but you can skip the phone number and fax boxes if you want.

**15.** Click Letter and **G**lossary to store the address so that you can use it again. The address is inserted in your letter.

**Address the letter to:**

Choose a title here ——

Mr.
Mr.
Ms.
Miss

**Full Name:**

**Suffix:**

Click in the box to type the
required information

**Position:**

**Company:**

**Address 1:**

**Address 2:**

**City:**

**State:**     **Zip Code:**

**Phone Number:**          **Acct/Doc ID# :**

**Fax Number:**

Click here to add to the letter
and store for future use ——

Place Address in:

**Letter and Glossary**     **Letter Only**     **Glossary Only**

**Cancel**

Word does miraculous, automatic things to add names and addresses to
your letter, and concludes by showing you the Notations box. This enables you to insert special notations such as Typist Initials, if you want.
Just leave these blank to skip them. Click OK to continue.

Word positions the insertion point at the beginning of the first text
paragraph. Type away! Check spelling and grammar, if you want. Then
save and print the letter.

**"I HATE THIS!"**

### I just remembered! I typed my old phone number in the Sender Information box!

Don't worry, you can easily correct this or any other information in the Sender Information box. With the template
document on-screen, open the Forma**t** menu and choose
Set Letter Options. You see the Letter options dialog box.
Click the Sender Info button, and you see the Enter Sender

Information dialog box again. Make your corrections or additions and click OK. Click **C**onfirm to confirm your changes, or click **E**dit to see the Enter Sender Information box again. Then click **C**lose.

### Top Ten Least Popular Letter Openings

**10.** "I promised I wouldn't bother you about this again, but…"

**9.** "You probably didn't realize someone was watching you when…"

**8.** "Get out your Visa card, because for $59.95 you can learn about an amazing home business opportunity stuffing envelopes…"

**7.** "Did you know that the possession of gerbils (a hamster relative) is still illegal in some states? The Rodent Rights League needs your help…"

**6.** "You probably don't remember me, but we dated in junior high school, and for some reason I can't get you out of my mind…"

**5.** "We have examined your 1992 return and propose the following adjustments…"

**4.** "An unauthorized charge in the amount of $4,351.19 was made to your credit card on April 22, 1993, in Lahore, Pakistan, and we are currently negotiating with the World Bank for the return of your funds. Unfortunately…"

**3.** "Even though you flunked out of Stagnant Water State University, we would still like you to consider contributing to our alumni fund…"

*continues*

**Top Ten Least Popular Letter Openings, continued**

**2.** "We appreciate the opportunity to review your manuscript, but…"

**1.** "The search committee has completed its deliberations, and we are sorry to inform you that…"

## Creating Additional Letters

After you fill out the sender information, creating additional letters is a breeze. You just click open the **F**ile menu, choose **N**ew, and pick a letter template.

**1.** Click OK to allow Word to set up the template with your sender information.

**2.** Select if you will use preprinted letterhead or blank paper.

**3.** Accept the edit feature by clicking OK.

You quickly see the Letter Addresser dialog box.

If you are going to send the letter to a person whose address you haven't filled out before, choose **N**ew and fill out the Address the letter to information, as you did previously.

If you are going to send the letter to a person whose name and address is already stored, do the following:

**1.** In the Letter Addresser dialog box, choose **G**lossary.

**2.** Pick the person's name from the list (it will be listed as *Name:* followed by the last name and the first initial, as in *Name: SledgeD*).

**3.** Click OK. You see the person's address information, which you can edit or complete. You always have a chance to edit the person's information before adding the name and address to your letter.

**4.** If you changed or expanded the information, click Letter and Glossary (and click **Y**es when you're asked if you want to redefine the existing glossary). If you didn't edit the information, click Letter Only.

**5.** Type the letter, check the spelling, save it, and print it!

**EXPERTS ONLY**

### Send the same letter to someone else!

Here's a neat trick. Suppose you've just finished writing and printing a letter, and you want to send the letter to another person. You can get Word to put in a different address. The name and address can be one that you've already typed and stored, or a new address that Word will store and add to your name and address list.

With the letter on-screen, open the Forma**t** menu and choose Insert Address. Click **Y**es to confirm replacing the address. You see the Letter Addresser dialog box. Click **G**lossary to choose an existing name and address from the list. Select a name from the list and click OK. When you see the Address the letter to: dialog box, just click **L**etter Only to add the name and address to the letter. (If you want to edit the information, do so and then click Letter and **G**lossary.)

Click **N**ew to see the Address the letter to: dialog box, and fill out the information. Click Letter and **G**lossary to save the information as well as place it in your letter.

# Creating Envelopes

When I get a letter, I can tell right away whether the sender is using a PC. Inside, the letter is nicely formatted with pretty fonts and all that jazz. But on the envelope, my name and address are scrawled out by hand. To get around this problem, I know people who have old, clunky manual typewriters next to their computers just to type envelopes!

Many of today's printers, especially laser and inkjet printers, have special envelope-loading slots that you can use to print envelopes. Even better, Word has a special envelope tool that makes printing envelopes a breeze.

To create an envelope for your letter, follow these steps:

**1.** With your completed letter on-screen (the one you created using one of Word's letter templates), click the Envelope tool on the Toolbar. You'll see the Create Envelope dialog box. Word has automatically added the names and addresses!

**2.** If you're using a company envelope that has a printed return address, click **O**mit Return Address.

**3.** If the envelope size is incorrect, click the down arrow in the Envelope size area and choose from a multitude of sizes.

**4.** Position the envelope in your printer's envelope slot. If you're not sure how to do this, take a look at your printer's manual—or better yet, get someone to show you how.

**5.** Click **P**rint Envelope.

**"I HATE THIS!"**

## It printed on the back of the envelope!

I know how this feels, because this just happened to me while I was testing the instructions you just read. Next time, turn the envelope over when you insert it into the printer.

# Creating a Fax Cover Sheet ("I heard it through the fax line...")

Fax machines are wonderful. You dial the person's fax machine number, stuff the pages into your fax machine, and press Send. At the other end, what you sent—graphics and all—comes out on that slimy fax paper (unless they have one of those cool but expensive plain-paper faxes). With or without the slimy paper, the fax is great.

If you've created your letter with Word's letter templates, you can crank out a cool-looking fax cover sheet that automatically includes your name and address, as well as your phone and fax numbers, and the name, address, and numbers of the person to whom you're sending the fax. Why send a cover sheet? If there are any problems with the transmission, the people at the other end know whom to call.

To create and print a cover sheet, follow these steps:

**1.** With your completed letter on-screen (the one you created using one of Word's letter templates), click open the Format menu and choose Create Fax Cover Sheet. You see the Fax Cover Sheet dialog box. Word has added all or most of the information automatically.

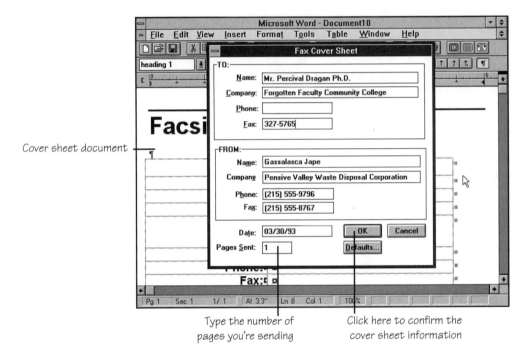

Cover sheet document

Type the number of
pages you're sending

Click here to confirm the
cover sheet information

**2.** In the Pages Sent box, type the total number of pages you are going
to send, including the cover sheet.

**3.** Click OK. Word adds the information to the fax cover sheet and
displays a dialog box informing you that you've created a new
document for your fax sheet. To see your letter again, you need to
choose the document from the **Window** menu.

**4.** Click OK to close this information dialog box. Now you can see
the fax cover sheet, which is an ordinary Word document now.
You can add to it and print it as you want.

**5.** If you want to add comments to the fax cover sheet, add them in the Comments area. If any of the needed information is missing, type it now.

**6.** To print your cover sheet, click open the **File** menu and choose **Print**, or just click the Print tool.

**7.** Close the document without saving it (it has served its purpose) and return to your letter.

Once upon...

a timeframe,

WHAT'RE YOU DOING?

WORKING.

LOOKS LIKE YOU'RE SITTING.

I'M TRYING TO WRITE, IF YOU REALLY MUST KNOW.

WHAT'RE YOU WRITING?

NOTHING, SO FAR.

BUT THE COMPUTER MAKES WRITING A LOT EASIER, I'LL SAY THAT.

WITH JUST A FLICK OF THE FINGER...

I CAN WRITE REAMS OF NOTHING.

WHIRRRRR

I CALL IT "STREAM OF UNCONSCIOUSNESS."

# CHAPTER 13

# Put It in a List

## IN A NUTSHELL

▼ Create a regular list

▼ Sort a list

▼ Add bullets without violating firearm laws

▼ Get Word to number your list while you relax sipping a Coke

L ists are a big part of life—laundry lists, Top Ten lists, enemy lists. Word gives you great tools for making lists. You can sort your lists and automatically add bullets (little marks that set off each item of the list). Word can even number the items in your list automatically. Forget those grade-school lessons in counting and alphabetization—let Word do it for you!

# List It

Items in a list are usually indented. You can indent lists by selecting all the paragraphs and clicking the Nest Paragraph tool on the Toolbar, but the best way is to create a hanging indent.

**BUZZWORDS**

**HANGING INDENT**

A hanging indent is a paragraph format. The first line is flush to the left margin, whereas the second and subsequent lines are indented. On the first line, you can make the text go all the way to the left margin; however, the more common practice is to put a bullet (a mark like a big, thick dot) or a number flush to the margin, so that all the text looks indented.

**TIP**

If you're planning to create a bulleted or numbered list (a hanging indent with little dots or numbers at the beginning of each paragraph), don't bother formatting the hanging indent manually. As described later in this chapter, you can use the cool Numbered List or Bulleted List tools to enter not only the numbers and bullets (in any caliber you want), but also to create the hanging indent.

If you're thinking about making a two-column list, stop thinking of it as a list and start thinking of it as a table—and flip to Chapter 14.

▼ The easiest way to create a hanging indent is to select one or more paragraphs and use the Ctrl+T keyboard shortcut (hold down the Ctrl key and press T, uppercase or lowercase). Word keeps the first line flush to the left margin, but indents the second and subsequent lines 0.5 inches.

▼ If you want to increase the hanging indent, press Ctrl+T again. With every press of Ctrl+T, you get an additional 0.5 inch indentation for the second and subsequent lines (the first line stays flush-left).

▼ To decrease the hanging indent by one tab stop, press Ctrl+G. With every press of Ctrl+G, you remove one half inch from the hanging indentation.

# Sort It

As long as you've created your list with each item in a separate paragraph, you can get Word to sort the list. You can sort alphanumerically (numbers first, then letters), numerically, or by date, as explained in the checklist. You can sort in ascending or descending order.

I HATE WORD FOR WINDOWS!

**BUZZWORDS**

**ASCENDING and DESCENDING**

When you sort in ascending order, Word sorts letters like this: a, b, c. It sorts numbers like this: 1, 2, 3. When you sort in descending order, Word sorts letters like this: z, x, y. It sorts numbers like this: infinity, googol, biggie. Actually, you already know about *descending numerical order* from our Top Ten lists, which start with number 10.

To sort your list, follow these steps:

**1.** Very important: Select just the stuff you want to sort. If you don't do this, Word will try to sort your entire document, the results of which would be humorous if they weren't catastrophic.

**2.** Open the Tools menu and choose Sorting. You see the Sorting dialog box.

Choose the sort order here —

Choose the sort type here —

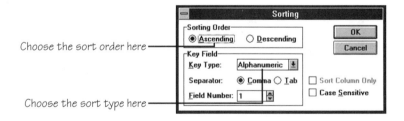

**3.** In the Sorting Order area, choose the sorting order you want— Ascending (the default) or Descending.

**4.** In the Key Field area, choose the sort type you want in the **Key Type** text box (Alphanumeric, Numeric, or Date). Forget about all the rest of this stuff in this area unless you want to give up being a writer and become a computer programmer instead.

**5.** If you want Word to pay a little attention to case (capital letters) when it sorts, click Case Sensitive. This makes Word put the capitalized items before the words that start with the same lowercase letters (Abraxas, abacus, Barbie, baby goat, Clinton, chums).

**6.** Click OK or press Enter. Word sorts what you selected. Hope it worked out OK.

**"I HATE THIS!"**

### It didn't work right!

If your sort goes awry for some reason (for instance, you chose the wrong sort order or type), immediately click open the Edit menu and choose Undo Sort.

# Bullet It

Bulleted lists look great when you want to list several items without suggesting that they're in any kind of order of importance. Thanks to the Bulleted List tool on the Ruler, it's really easy to create a bulleted list with Word.

**TIP**

If you're typing a single-spaced document, you'll find that items in a bulleted list look best when they're separated by a blank line. To add a blank line to each paragraph in the list, select the paragraphs and press Ctrl+O (the letter).

To create a bulleted list, follow these steps:

**1.** Type each item in its own paragraph. Don't bother setting up the hanging indent or adding the bullets; Word does these things for you.

**2.** Select the items.

**3.** Click the Bulleted List tool on the Toolbar. You see the results.

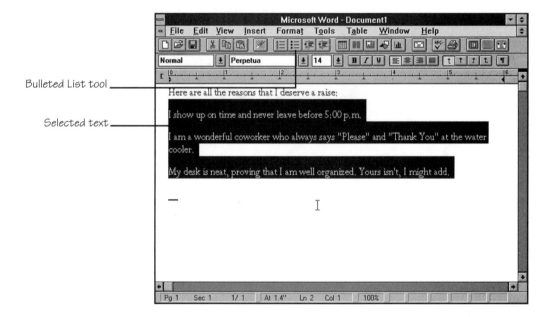

Bulleted List tool ————

Selected text ————

"I HATE THIS!"

### I don't like it! I want to get rid of it!

OK, no problem. Select the list again, click open the **Tools** menu, and choose **Bullets and Numbering**. Click **Remove**. Gone!

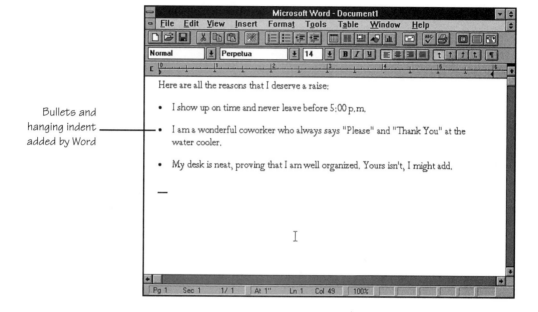

Bullets and hanging indent added by Word

**EXPERTS ONLY**

## Choosing a higher-caliber bullet

When you use the Bulleted List tool, Word uses the current settings in the Bullets and Numbering dialog box. If you like, you can choose a different bullet. Select the paragraphs you just bulleted, open the Tools menu, and choose Bullets and Numbering. You'll see the Bullets and Numbering dialog box. Click a different bullet. You can also change the bullet's point size or change the amount of the hanging indent (0.25 inch by default). When you are finished choosing options, click OK or press Enter. The bullet you selected becomes the default.

If you want to add another item to a list, it's simple. At the end of the list, press Enter to start a new paragraph, and click the Bulleted List

I HATE WORD FOR WINDOWS!

button. Word adds the bullet at the beginning of the paragraph, creates the hanging indent format, and positions the insertion point so that you can just start typing the text.

# Number It

You can use numbered lists to put items in rank order (like our Top Ten lists do), or you can use them for instructions. Instead of typing the numbers yourself (a detestable activity), let Word do it.

To create a numbered list, follow these steps:

1. Type each item in its own paragraph. Don't bother setting up the hanging indent; Word does it for you.

2. Select the items.

3. Click the Numbered List tool on the Toolbar. You see the results.

**"I HATE THIS!"**

### I don't like this either! I want to get rid of it!

OK, no problem. Select the list again, click open the Tools menu, and choose Bullets and Numbering. Click Remove. Gone!

**EXPERTS ONLY**

### Choosing another numbering scheme

When you use the Numbered List tool, Word uses the current settings in the Bullets and Numbering dialog box. If you like, you can choose a different numbering scheme. Select the paragraphs you just bulleted, open the Tools menu, and

choose **B**ullets and Numbering. You'll see the Bullets and Numbering dialog box. In the **F**ormat list box, you can choose Roman numerals (I, II, III, IV, and so on, in upper- or lowercase) or alphabetical (A, B, C, D, and so on, in upper- or lowercase) When you are finished choosing options, click OK or press Enter.

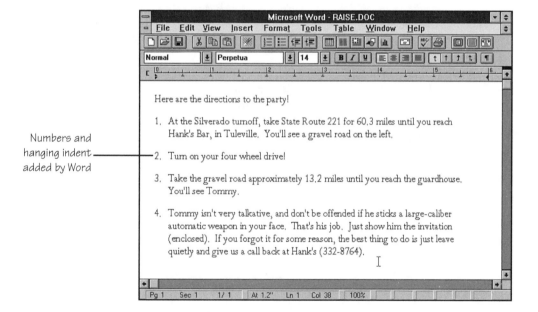

Numbers and hanging indent added by Word

You can easily add another item to the list. At the end of the list, press Enter to start a new paragraph, and click the Numbered List button. Word adds the correct number at the beginning of the paragraph (amazing, isn't it?), creates the hanging indent format, and positions the insertion point so that you can just start typing the text.

If you add an item in the middle of the list or switch items around, you need to renumber the items. Just select the text that is numbered and click the Numbered List button. The text will be properly renumbered.

**Top Ten Top Ten Lists Your Boss Shouldn't See**

**10.** Top Ten Resemblances between Our Boss and Attila the Hun

**9.** Our Top Ten Marketing Claims That Just Aren't True

**8.** Top Ten Ways of Sneaking into the Office Late Without Anyone Seeing

**7.** Top Ten Key Words and Phrases That Make It Sound Like You Fit in with Our Corporate Culture When You Really Don't

**6.** Top Ten Subjects That Are Sure to Derail Serious Discussion in Any Planning Meeting Whose Goals You Don't Like

**5.** Top Ten Customer Complaints That Have a Foundation in Fact

**4.** Top Ten Ways to Prolong a Business Trip without Raising Questions from the Accounting Department

**3.** Top Ten Ways to Take Credit for Someone Else's Work.

**2.** Top Ten Other People to Blame when Something Goes Wrong.

**1.** Top Ten Ways of Reprogramming the Boss's Performance Evaluation Spreadsheet So That It Always Gives You a "Superior" Rating

# CHAPTER 14

# Table It

## IN A NUTSHELL

- ▼ Insert a table
- ▼ Type text within a table
- ▼ Select text within a table
- ▼ Change the table layout
- ▼ Make a title for your table
- ▼ Sort the table rows
- ▼ Add borders and grids to a table
- ▼ Sum up numbers in table rows and columns

**M**any documents are enhanced by tables that give the details of trends such as rising sales, growing profits, and increased survival rates for office plants. Word provides some great tools for creating tables. Don't mess around with tabs: Create a table instead.

# What's a Table?

Within Word, a table is a grid that has columns and rows. It looks a little bit like a spreadsheet (if you are familiar with spreadsheet programs). When a column and row come together, the resulting square space is called a *cell*.

So what's so great about tables? A cell gets bigger when you type. I know, this doesn't sound like anything to start breathing heavily about. But compare it to typing a table with tabs. If the thing you're typing won't fit on the line, you have to start a new line and tab over. And, if you later make additions or deletions within the table, you can throw all the tab spacing completely out of whack, leading to frustration, destruction of valuable computer equipment, and finally, delirium.

There are no tabs in tables. That's a good sign, isn't it? Sure, you can set tabs within a table if you just insist. But you don't really need them. As far as Word is concerned, the text inside each table cell is its own, independent paragraph, which you can format just like any paragraph. For example, you can center the text within the cell, or whatever. And, it's easy to jazz up the table by adding lines, shading, and borders.

# Inserting the Table

As usual with Word, you can create tables in many different ways. The easiest way is to use that cunning little Table tool on the Toolbar.

**TIP**

> If you've already typed a tabbed table, there's no need to type the whole thing over again. Just select all the tabbed text, open the Table menu, and choose Convert Text to Table. Word quickly creates a table based on the number of lines and tabbed columns in the text you selected.

To create a table, follow these steps:

**1.** Decide how many columns and rows you need.

**2.** Click the Table tool on the Toolbar, and drag down until you have highlighted the number of columns and rows you want. To make more columns or rows available, just drag down (rows) or to the right (columns). When you've selected the number of columns and rows you want, release the mouse button. Word creates the table.

After you create the table, you'll notice that the Ruler changes; the big *T* marks show where the column boundaries are. You also see left and first-line indent marks for the cell in which the insertion point is positioned. The rows and columns are delineated by an on-screen grid, but this doesn't print. (You can, however, add borders that include an optional printing grid, if you like this effect. This is discussed later in this chapter.)

Table tool

7 x 3 Table

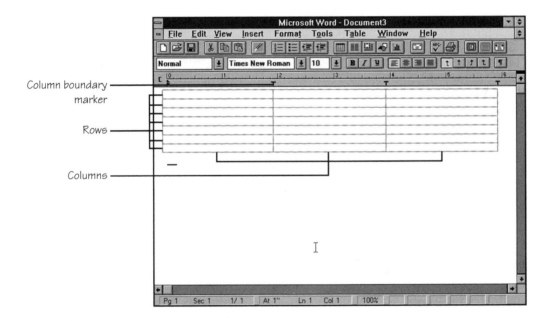

Column boundary marker

Rows

Columns

"I HATE THIS!"

## I didn't create the right number of rows!

Don't worry. You can easily add more rows or delete unwanted rows. And, it's easy to delete unwanted columns. It's a little tougher to insert columns, though, so if you didn't put in enough columns, open the **E**dit menu and choose **U**ndo to cancel the table insertion. Then try again.

# Typing Text in the Table

Now for the easy part. To type in a cell, just click within it and type. Word creates a default paragraph (single-spaced and flush left, with the default font and font size).

**TIP**

If you want to reformat all the table text, type the table, then open the Table menu and choose Select Table. This selects the entire table. Now you can choose the fonts and font sizes you want.

The following shows a three-column table with six rows. I have chosen classy formatting to disguise the fact that the table contains no reliable information.

A three-column table to keep track of fashion trends in South Dakota.

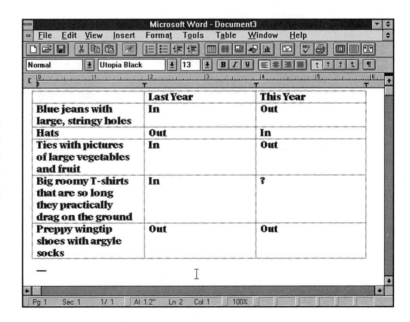

|  | Last Year | This Year |
|---|---|---|
| Blue jeans with large, stringy holes | In | Out |
| Hats | Out | In |
| Ties with pictures of large vegetables and fruit | In | Out |
| Big roomy T-shirts that are so long they practically drag on the ground | In | ? |
| Preppy wingtip shoes with argyle socks | Out | Out |

193

I HATE WORD FOR WINDOWS!

**TIP**

If you're at the end of a table and still have another row (or more) to type, just position the insertion point at the end of the row (past the text, if any), and press Tab. Lo! Word creates another row.

**CAUTION**

Be aware that, within a table, the Tab key doesn't work like it normally does. Instead, it advances the selection to the next cell. If there isn't a next cell, pressing Tab creates a new row, a matter that was the subject of a recent Tip.

## Selecting within a Table

Need to format the text in the table? Insert a row within the table? Adjust the column boundaries? The key is selecting rows and columns first.

**Selecting stuff in a table**

▼ To select all the text in a single cell, move the pointer to the cell's selection bar (yes, a cell has its very own selection bar, which is next to the left cell boundary) and click.

▼ To select two or more cells, select one cell and then drag to the adjacent cell or cells.

▼ To select a row, put the insertion point in one of the row's cells. Then open the Table menu and choose Select **R**ow. If you prefer using the mouse, move the pointer to the selection bar next to the row, then click the left mouse button.

▼   To select more than one row, move the pointer to the selection bar next to the first row, then drag down or up.

▼   To select a column, put the insertion point in one of the column's cells. Then open the Table menu and choose Select Column. If you prefer to use the mouse, move the pointer to the top cell border in the column until a cute little down arrow appears. Then click the left mouse button. Alternatively, you can position the cursor anywhere in the column and press the right mouse button, which then highlights the entire column.

▼   To select more than one column, move the pointer to the top cell border in the column until the down arrow appears. Then drag right or left to select the current column and additional columns.

# Inserting and Deleting Columns and Rows

Word's ordinary deletion commands (such as Cut in the Edit menu and the Del key) work for text, but not the table grid. If you want to change the table layout by inserting or deleting columns and rows, you need the special techniques described in the following, extra-handy checklist.

### Playing havoc with columns and rows

▼   To delete a column, select it. (You can select more than one column.) Then open the Table menu and choose Delete Columns.

▼   To delete a row, select it. (You can select more than one row.) Then open the Table menu and choose Delete Rows.

*continues*

▼ To insert a row, select where you want the inserted row to be placed. (Same old thing—you can insert more than one row.) Then open the Table menu and choose **Insert Rows**.

▼ To insert a column, select where you want the inserted column to be placed. (This is getting old by now, I know, but you can select more than one column.) Then open the Table menu and choose **Insert Columns**. Note: After inserting a new column, you have to adjust the column width to keep the table from going over the right margin. How? Read on.

▼ To adjust column width, carefully move the pointer to the column boundary until the pointer changes shape (you see two vertical lines with arrows pointing left and right). Then drag the column boundary in the desired direction (I mean, as long as it's left or right).

# Titling the Table (Sir Table)

To add a title to the table, follow these steps:

**1.** Select the first row of your table.

**2.** If necessary, open the Table menu and choose **Insert Rows** to create a nice, blank row at the top of your table.

**3.** With the new row still selected, open the Table menu and choose **Merge Cells**. This gives you one big, happy cell in which to put your title.

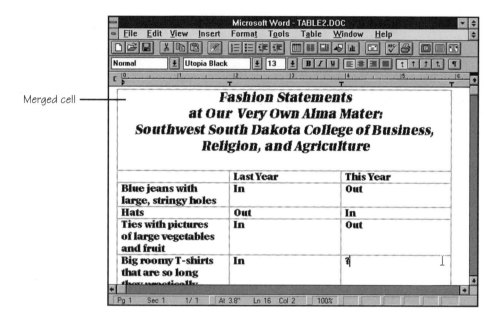

Merged cell —

| | Last Year | This Year |
|---|---|---|
| Blue jeans with large, stringy holes | In | Out |
| Hats | Out | In |
| Ties with pictures of large vegetables and fruit | In | Out |
| Big roomy T-shirts that are so long | In | ? |

**"I HATE THIS!"**

## I can't get rid of this table!

Tables hang on tenaciously to life. If you really want to remove the whole thing from your document, select the whole table (open the Table menu and choose Select Table). Then choose Convert Table to Text. When the Convert Table to Text dialog box appears, just click OK or press Enter to convert the table to a tabbed table.

### Top Ten Tables You Can Throw into Your Reports to Keep the Competition Off Balance

**10.** Seasonal Breakdown of Ronco Corporation's Veg-O-Matic Sales

**9.** Your Chances of Being Killed in a Freak Accident

*continues*

**Top Ten Tables You Can Throw into Your Reports to
Keep the Competition Off Balance, continued**

**8.** Class and Income Breakdown of Patients with Ingrown Toenails

**7.** Patterns and Trends in Elvis Sightings: Is He Leaving a Trail?

**6.** Effect of Heavy Metal and Hip-Hop on Three Species of House
Plants

**5.** Areas That You'd Never Believe Are Prone to Earthquakes,
but Are

**4.** Percentage of National Enquirer Readers Who Watch Daytime
Television

**3.** Does Familiarity Breed Contempt? Look at the Facts

**2.** Geographical Patterns in Cajun Pork Rind Consumption

**1.** State-by-State Breakdown of Lonely Highways Implicated in UFO
Abductions

# Sorting a Table

The previous chapter introduced Word's sorting capabilities, which you
unleashed on innocent paragraphs within a list. You can also sort table
rows. This is great for putting a table into alphabetical, numerical, or
chronological order really fast.

The trick here is to select the column you want Word to sort by before
choosing the Sorting command. Selecting just these cells tells Word, in

effect, "Put the rows of this table in order, and use the stuff in this column to determine the order."

**TIP**

Remember this neat fact: Unlike paragraphs, table rows don't have to be sorted by the first thing in them. If the fourth column of your table is titled *Date*, and you want to arrange the rows by date, fine. Just select the cells of that column in the rows you want sorted.

To sort the table after selecting the column cells to sort by, open the Tools menu and choose Sorting. In the Sorting Order and Key Field areas, choose the sorting order and sorting type you want. But please, don't click Sort Column Only! If you do, Word scrambles your data. Click OK or press Enter to do the sort.

# Adding Borders to a Table

Chapter 10 introduced Word's Border command, which enables you to add lines, boxes, and shading to paragraphs. When you use it with a table, this command takes on a new dimension, because it becomes possible to add printing grid lines over the nonprinting grid lines you see on-screen.

To put a box around your table and add grid lines within all the selected cells, just select the cells, open the Format menu, and choose **B**order. In the Border Cells dialog box, click **G**rid, and click OK.

You can also add lines above, below, to the left, or to the right of the cell, as you can with borders. You can also add shading. For more information about adding lines and shading, flip to Chapter 10.

# It All Adds Up

Word isn't a spreadsheet program, but you can quickly add up totals for rows and columns. If you're planning to use this nice feature, leave a blank column at the right of your table, or a blank row at the bottom, to hold the sums.

To add up the cells in a row or column, select the cells. (You have to do this one row or one column at a time.) Then open the Tools menu and choose Calculate. Word shows the sum on the status bar. To insert it in a cell, place the insertion point in the cell and click the Paste tool on the Toolbar or press Shift+Insert. What could be easier?

# CHAPTER 15

# Say It with a Picture

## IN A NUTSHELL

▼ Add clip art pictures to
   your document
▼ Crop and scale pictures
▼ Draw your own pictures
   with Microsoft Draw

No matter what, I will not begin this chapter with the tired, old cliché: "A picture is worth a thousand words." The saying is out-of-date, anyway. As everyone knows on Madison Avenue these days, a good picture is worth a thousand bucks, at least. But for surprisingly little effort, you can incorporate pictures into your Word documents. Word comes with a few picture files that you can insert in your Word documents, and you can buy additional picture file packages.

If you can't find exactly the picture you need to get your point across, you can create your own, using Word's drawing capabilities, which are pretty neat. Microsoft Draw is a good drawing program that comes with Word; you can use it to create good-looking drawings and illustrations.

# Adding Clip Art

The correct word for picture files, incidentally, is *clip art*.

**BUZZWORDS**

**CLIP ART**

A collection of pictures, one to a file, that you can add to your documents. The files are stored in one of several file formats, such as Computer Graphics Metafile (.CGM) or Windows Bitmap (.BMP). Word can read almost any graphics file format.

To insert a clip art picture into your document, follow these steps:

**1.** Place the insertion point where you want the picture to appear.

**2.** Open the **Insert** menu and choose **Picture**. You see the Picture dialog box. Basically, this is just an Open dialog box with a few additions that pertain to graphics files.

Find the clipart directory here ——

Choose a file here ——

Click here to preview the picture ——

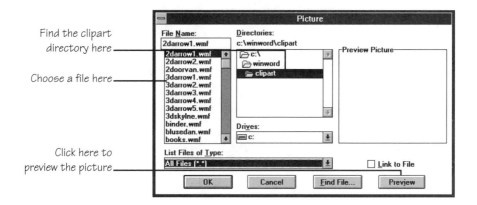

**3.** Use the Directories list box to open the directory that contains the clip art. You'll find some sample clip art files in the *clipart* directory, which is a subdirectory of the Word directory.

**4.** Select a picture by clicking on a file name.

**5.** If you want to see a preview of your picture, click Preview.

**6.** To add the picture to your document, click OK or press Enter. You see the picture in your document.

**TIP**

Word adds the picture to your document in the form of a frame, which is a rectangular area bounded by nonprinting borders. To position the frame on the page, click one of the alignment buttons on the Ruler.

A picture added to a Word document (from Presentation Task Force, New Vision Technologies, Inc.).

## Top Ten Least Popular Clip Art Collections

**10.** Portraits of Losing Vice Presidential Candidates

**9.** Vistas from Urban New Jersey

**8.** Landscapes Collection XIII: Hazardous Waste Dumps

**7.** Popes with Beards

**6.** The Household Insect Collection

**5.** Toes of the Rich and Famous

**4.** The Chicken: From Beak to Tailfeather

**3.** Scenes from the Crypt

# Cropping and Scaling Pictures

No, this section doesn't deal with the latest agricultural techniques. In it, you learn how to chop off the parts of the picture you don't want to reveal to the masses, as well as how to *size* the picture (enlarge it or reduce it).

**BUZZWORDS**

**CROPPING and SCALING**

When you *crop* a picture, you reduce its size without shrinking the picture, so that some of the picture isn't visible. You can do this to hide the parts you don't want to display. To *scale* a graphic means to enlarge or reduce the graphic's size without cropping it or hiding anything.

## Crop, Crop, Crop

To crop your picture, follow these steps:

**1.** Click the picture to select it. You see the sizing handles (the little gray boxes).

**2.** Hold down the Shift key and drag one of the sizing handles.

Sizing handles

"I HATE THIS!"

### It looks awful! I wish I hadn't done that!

Don't panic. Just open the **E**dit menu and choose **U**ndo Picture Formatting, or just press Ctrl+Z.

## One Size Doesn't Fit All

To size your picture, follow these steps:

**1.** Click the picture to select it. You see the sizing handles.

**2.** Drag one of the sizing handles. If the picture looks worse, open the **E**dit menu and choose **U**ndo Picture Formatting, or just press Ctrl+Z.

▼      Want to copy or move your picture? You can do so using the copying or moving techniques discussed in Chapter 2. Just select the picture, and then copy or move it using the mouse or the Clipboard. For more information about copying and moving techniques, flip to Chapter 2.

▼      If you don't like your picture and want to get rid of it, you can do so easily enough. Just select the picture and press Del.

# Draw Your Own!

Can't find the right clip art picture to get your point across? You can draw your own with Microsoft Draw, an accessory application that is packaged with Word.

With Draw, you can use a variety of tools to create lines, ovals and circles, rectangles and squares, arcs and polygons (shapes with many sides). For each of these shapes, you can choose a line thickness, line color, and fill color or pattern. After entering any shape, you can select it independently and then crop it or size it as you please.

To create your own drawing, follow these steps:

**1.** Position the insertion point where you want your drawing to appear.

**2.** Click the Drawing tool on the Ruler. You see the Microsoft Draw window.

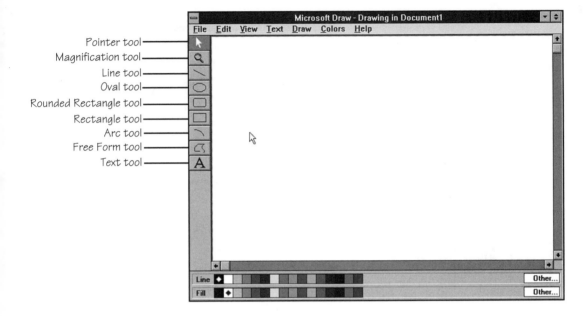

Pointer tool
Magnification tool
Line tool
Oval tool
Rounded Rectangle tool
Rectangle tool
Arc tool
Free Form tool
Text tool

**3.** Click one of the drawing tools and start your drawing. For the lowdown on the drawing tools, see the upcoming checklist.

**4.** When you are finished making your drawing, open the **File** menu and choose **Update**. This puts your picture in the Word document. Then click **Exit and Return**.

**"I HATE THIS!"**

## It's asking whether I want to update the Word document!

You probably forget to choose **Update** from the **File** menu before exiting Microsoft Draw. Click **Yes** to update the Word document (this means, "Place the drawing in the Word document").

## The drawing tools

▼   The Pointer or Selection tool selects text or objects in your draw-ing in order to edit them in some way. You can select multiple objects by holding down the Shift and Ctrl keys and clicking on the objects.

▼   Click the Magnifying Glass tool to get a closer view of your work. This helps when you're trying to get lines to join nicely. To restore the default view, open the **V**iew menu and choose **F**ull Size.

▼   Click the Line tool to make a line. After clicking the tool, move the crosshairs to the place you want the line to start, and drag to make the line. Release the mouse button to stop drawing the line. To make a straight vertical or horizontal line, hold down the Shift key while dragging.

▼   Click the Oval tool to make an oval or circle. After clicking the tool, move the crosshairs to the place you want one corner of the oval to be, then click and drag diagonally to make the oval. To make a perfect circle, hold down the Shift key while you drag.

▼   Click the Rounded Rectangle or Rectangle tools to make a rect-angle. After clicking the tool, move the crosshairs to the place you want one corner of the rectangle to be, then click and drag diago-nally to make the rectangle. To make a perfect square, hold down the Shift key while you drag.

▼   Click the Arc tool to make an arc or wedge shape. To make an arc, open the **D**raw menu and deselect the **F**illed option; if you leave this option on, you get a wedge shape that looks like a slice of pie. To make the arc or wedge, click in your drawing and then drag to make the shape. To make an arc that is a section of a perfect circle, hold down the Shift key while you drag.

*continues*

▼ Click the Free Form tool to make a line drawing made out of straight line sections. To make the shape, click within your drawing and drag to form the first segment, then click. Drag again to form the second segment, and click. To finish drawing the shape, double-click.

▼ Click the Text tool to enter text in your drawing. You can enter only one line of text at a time. After clicking the tool, move the insertion point to where you want the text to appear, and click. Then type the text. To format the text, click the Pointer tool, select the text box, and choose formats from the **T**ext menu. (You can choose styles such as bold, italic, and underline; left, center, and right alignments; and fonts and font sizes.) Note: To edit the text after you insert it, open the **E**dit menu and choose **E**dit Text (or just use the Ctrl+E keyboard shortcut).

▼ You can choose line thicknesses, line colors, and fill colors or patterns after creating the shape. Just click the shape to select it. To choose a pattern, open the **D**raw menu and choose **P**attern, and select a pattern from the popup menu. To choose a line style (including dotted lines, dashed lines, and various line thicknesses), open the **D**raw menu, choose Line Style, and choose a style from the popup menu. To choose a line or fill color, just click a color in the palettes at the bottom of the screen.

▼ To size any shape you have entered, click it to select it, then drag one of the handles. To move the shape, click within the middle of the shape and hold down the mouse button until dotted lines appear. Then drag the shape.

▼ You can flip and rotate any shape. To do so, select it, open the **D**raw menu, and choose Rotate/Flip. When the popup menu appears, you can choose to rotate the shape left or right, or flip it horizontally or vertically.

I HATE WORD FOR WINDOWS!

**TIP**

As you make your drawing, you'll find that you can put new shapes "on top" of old ones. If you cover up a shape but need to edit it, use the Bring to **F**ront and Send to **B**ack commands (on the **E**dit menu) to make a shape accessible.

**"I HATE THIS!"**

### I added the picture to my document, but I need to change it. How do I edit it?

It's really simple. Just double-click it. Word starts Microsoft Draw and displays your picture. Now you can edit it as you want. To update the drawing in your document, open the **F**ile menu and choose **U**pdate. Then open the **F**ile menu and choose **E**xit and Return.

# CHAPTER 16

# Timesaving Tricks: Glossaries, Styles, and Templates

## IN A NUTSHELL

▼ Store and retrieve text for repeated use

▼ Store two or more formats as a style and apply them *en masse*

▼ Create templates that make your styles available for new documents

The true moment of mastery of any software program is when, groveling in submission, the program begs, "Yes, master, yes, I'll do exactly what you want, the way you want, and when you want." There is a certain psychological satisfaction to be derived from this, believe me.

So that's why we're talking about glossaries, styles, and templates in this chapter. I know you're thinking, "I've never heard of any of these things." Don't feel bad, but do read on. All three of these things are fantastic time-savers. And what's more, they're all ways you can customize Word so that it does things your way, rather than the other way around. They're easy to use, too, which ought to make the whole package irresistible.

## Repeat Yourself

Here's a good rule to remember: Never type the same stuff twice. If you believe that you can reuse a block of text (of any size, ranging from a few words to many pages), create a glossary.

**BUZZWORDS**

**GLOSSARY**

A chunk of text (which can include graphics) that you name and store so that you can retrieve it later.

Glossaries have many uses. Legal firms use them to construct legal documents out of collections of standard passages. Corporations use them to describe their mission or their products. Blackmailers use them to describe in detail what they will do if the payment isn't made.

# Creating the Glossary Entry

To create, name, and store your glossary entry, follow these steps:

**1.** In your document, select the text or graphics that you want to place in the glossary. A glossary entry can store borders, shading, fonts, pictures, and all the other stuff that you can use to prettify your text.

**2.** Open the **E**dit menu and choose Glossary. You see the Glossary dialog box. At the bottom of the box, the Selection area shows what you selected.

Type the glossary name here (31 characters maximum).

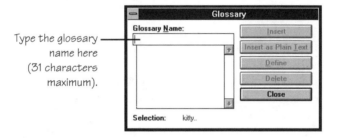

**3.** In the Glossary **N**ame box, type a name of up to 31 characters for the glossary you are creating. Be sure to choose a descriptive name that will enable you to choose the glossary from the list of names. You can include spaces.

**4.** Click **D**efine or press Enter.

You see your document again. That was easy, wasn't it?

**"I HATE THIS!"**

### The Glossary option is dimmed!

If the **Edit** menu's **Gl**ossary option is dimmed, it means that you haven't selected anything in your document. Select some text, then try again.

### Ideas for using glossaries

▼ Directions to your house

▼ A graphic that you like to insert in all your documents, such as a company logo or a picture of your cat

▼ A memo distribution list

▼ A carefully-worded, standard passage about something with legal implications, such as returns or warranties

▼ A report title that you use frequently, complete with fonts, font sizes, spacing after, and centered alignment

▼ Your company's address, telephone, and fax number, surrounded by a border and formatted with centered alignment

▼ A table format that you use repeatedly

▼ Carefully worked out, stock phrases ("boilerplate") for certain touchy things that come up again and again ("Of course we value your service to our firm, and your record is excellent! I can tell you this much—keep up the good work and that promotion you want is sure to come, in time.")

## Inserting the Glossary Entry

After you have created a glossary entry, you can insert it into any open document. Follow these steps to insert a glossary entry:

1. Place the insertion point where you want the glossary to appear.

2. Open the **E**dit menu and choose Glossary. You see the Glossary dialog box again.

3. In the list box, select the name of the glossary you want to insert.

4. Click **I**nsert (to insert the glossary with all the formatting, fonts, graphics, and extra stuff) or Insert as Plain **T**ext (to insert just the text without any formats, borders, or graphics).

**TIP**

You also can type the glossary name in the document, then press F3. Word inserts the text.

## Editing the Glossary Entry

Glossary entry need changing? That's easy enough. Just insert the glossary into a document, edit the entry, select it, and choose Glossary from the **E**dit menu. When you see the Glossary dialog box, select the glossary name in the list box and choose Define. You'll see a question box asking you whether you want to redefine the glossary entry. Click **Y**es.

## Saving the Glossary Entry

Glossaries aren't automatically saved when you create them. On the contrary, they're kept in Word's memory. If you just switch off your computer without closing Word properly and saving the glossaries you've created or edited, they're goners.

You get your big chance to save your glossaries when you exit Word. If there are any unsaved glossaries, you see a question box with the message Do you want to save the global glossary and command changes?. Click Yes.

**TIP**

Always click **Yes** when you see this dialog box, even if you're not sure whether the glossary you created is worth saving. It's much easier to delete an unneeded glossary than it is to reconstruct a lot of unsaved work. (To delete an unneeded glossary, open the **E**dit menu, choose Glossary, select the glossary you want to delete, and click Delete.)

**Top Ten Glossaries Found on Computer of Washington Lobbyist**

**10.** This little contribution just goes to show our appreciation for your patriotism, integrity, and public service…

**9.** Let me tell you about this little bank out in Phoenix that your son or daughter might want to run…

**8.** Of course we do represent certain foreign governments, but we believe everyone wins from the free flow of information…

**7.** There are just so many reasons why this program needs more funding, not less…

**6.** You wouldn't really want us to disclose the circumstances behind…

**5.** Nothing more than token gifts, this Rolls-Royce and Swiss Alps vacation are only meant to express our appreciation for your courage in that recent roll-call vote…

**4.** This map shows where we can meet and be sure that no one's listening…

**3.** We'd be happy to offer you a modest honorarium for your speech, say $250,000…

**2.** If you like, we think we can take care of those bounced checks…

**1.** Don't feel that you have to risk re-election by voting yourself a raise; there's a little something we can do to make up the difference…

# Styles of the Rich and Famous

Suppose you've been doing some real serious formatting. You've created an indented paragraph format for an extended quotation— you know, one of those things that's indented on both sides. Not to be outdone, you chose a smaller font size for this thing. It was a lot of work to create it.

What happens if you want to use the quote format again? You can copy it, but that's a hassle. Wouldn't it be nice if there were a way you could collect all those formats together, save them, name them, and apply them just by choosing the style's name from a list? Well, you can. The answer lies in Word's styles.

**BUZZWORDS**

**STYLE**

A collection of formats, which can include character formats (including a font, a font size, and an emphasis) and paragraph formats (including alignment, indents, and even stuff like borders and shading). When you create the style, you name it and store it. You can later apply it to text in documents.

What are styles for? Here are some ideas.

**Some uses for styles**

▼ A standard text paragraph that includes font, font size (12 points), a 0.5-inch first-line indent, justified alignment, and double-line spacing

▼ A standard subheading that includes font, font size (14 points), flush-left alignment, two blank lines before, one blank line after, and Keep With Next paragraph formatting so that Word doesn't leave the subheading all by itself at the bottom of a page

▼ An extended quotation format that indents the text from the left and from the right, and uses a font size smaller than the text paragraph font size

▼ A title format that centers the text, applies bold, uses a particularly garish font, and enlarges it to a font size that will leave an indelible impression on the mind of everyone who sees it

**TIP**

The easiest way to create and apply styles is to use the Ribbon. If you don't see the Ribbon on-screen, open the **View** menu and choose **Ribbon**.

## Creating the Style

Word comes with four styles already defined: Normal, Heading 1, Heading 2, and Heading 3. You've been using the default style, Normal style, all this time, haven't you? You use the Heading styles to create document titles, headings, and subheadings.

Rather than redefine the Normal style, it's better to create new styles for things such as body text paragraphs. The Normal style is a generic, no-fancy-stuff style that comes in handy sometimes, so it's best to leave it alone instead of adding things like indents or blank lines.

To create a style, create a paragraph that has all the formats you want. You can include any character or paragraph format you like, including fonts, font sizes, alignments, indents, borders, shading, tabs, and even frame positions (see Chapter 15 for the lowdown on positioning frames).

After you have formatted the paragraph, do the following:

**1.** Select the paragraph.

**2.** Double-click the style name in the style box on the Ribbon. This selects the name (Normal). Then type your new name for the style. You can type up to 24 characters. You can use spaces and special characters, with the exception of that nasty old backslash character that is so beloved by DOS users ( \ ).

Style box

| Normal | Times New Roman | 10 | **B** *I* U |

**3.** Click outside the style box to create the style. Simple!

"I HATE THIS!"

### Where's the style I created?

When you create a style, Word saves it along with the current document (the one that's on-screen when you create the style)—but no others. If you want to use the style in another document, you must copy the style to the other document in a procedure called *merging styles*. Another option (also discussed) is to create a template document that has all the styles you want, and then to use this template for future documents.

# Applying the Style

After you have created a style, you can apply it anywhere in your document. You can do so in two ways. If you apply the style to existing text, the style you apply replaces the existing text's formats. If you press Enter to start a new paragraph and then apply the style, you can start typing, and your text will have the style's formats.

To apply a style, just click the arrow next to the style box, and click the name of the style you want to apply. If the results prove disastrous, open the Edit menu and choose Undo Formatting, or just click Ctrl+Z.

# Redefining the Style

A major Good Thing about styles is that, when you change a style, your change affects all the paragraphs to which you have applied the style. Suppose you have defined a style for subheadings throughout your document. After printing the document, you decide that the font looks goofy, so you redefine the style. Automatically, the change applies to all the subheadings throughout the document—you don't have to go through your document page by page and make the change.

To redefine a style, follow these steps:

**1.** Select one of the paragraphs to which you have applied the style.

**2.** Change the formatting, using any of the usual techniques. For example, choose a new font or font size.

**3.** Click within the style box on the Ribbon and press Enter. You see a question box asking whether you want to redefine the style based on the selection.

**4.** Click **Y**es. Word redefines the style and automatically reformats all the paragraphs to which the style was applied.

**EXPERTS ONLY**

### More hot style tricks

The Style dialog box (displayed when you click **S**tyle in the Forma**t** menu) enables you to do several neat things, which nerdy types find irresistible. Here are just two that are especially keen: You can assign a style to a shortcut key using the Ctrl+Shift key combination. To do this, you use the Shortcut Key area of the Style dialog box. And, you can tell Word to apply a different style *after* you type with the

*continues*

> ## More hot style tricks, continued
>
> current style and press Enter. This is great when you've defined a style that will always be followed by another style. For example, you might want to define a Heading style and follow it with your Body Text style. To tell Word which style to apply after the current style, you use the Next Style list box in the Style dialog box.

# Merging Styles from Another Document

You're working on a new document. You want to use that nifty style you created. But it's not available. It lives only in the document where you created it. With the following cunning procedure, however, you can take the styles from another document and merge them with the current document's styles. After you do this, the style you want will be available in the current document.

To merge styles, follow these steps:

**1.** In the document to which you want to copy the style, open the Format menu and choose Style. You'll see the Style dialog box.

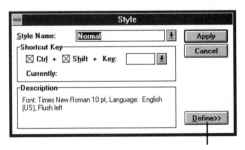

Click here to see more options

**2.** Click **D**efine. This enlarges the Style dialog box.

**3.** Click the **M**erge button. You see a Merge Styles dialog box, which is essentially an Open dialog box that is set up to retrieve styles.

**4.** Click down the List Files of **T**ype list, and choose Word Document (*.doc).

**5.** Locate the file that contains the styles you want to copy, and click OK or press Enter. You see a question box asking you to confirm this operation.

**6.** Click **Y**es.

**7.** In the Style dialog box, click Close to return to your document. The styles from the other document are now available.

# Tampering with Templates

Every Word document is based on a template. Templates, introduced in Chapter 12, are used to store the formats, styles, and other stuff such as macros that are suited to a particular kind of document, like a letter, memo, or report. Templates are actually like ordinary Word documents, except for one important thing: When you open a template, the template goes into an untitled document, which you save to a different file name. The good thing about this is that, when you save this document, you don't overwrite or mess up the stuff that's in the original template, so it's ready for your use next time.

If you have created many styles for a particular kind of document, such as a quarterly report or a poem, you will want to use these styles in many documents. By far the best way to save these styles for reuse is to create a

template. You can then create new documents based on this template, and Presto! Your styles become available. No merging, no fussing.

You can make a template out of an ordinary Word document—a document in which you have created all the styles you want the template to have.

## Saving a Document as a Template

To save a document as a template, follow these steps:

**1.** In your Word document, create all the styles you want the template to have.

**2.** Important! Save your document as a normal Word document (you'll see why in the next step).

**3.** Select all the text in the document, except the text (such as a return address, memo header, or "generic" title page) that you can use in every document you base on this template. Then press Del.

**4.** Open the **F**ile menu and choose Save **A**s. You see the Save As dialog box.

**5.** In the Save File as **T**ype list box, choose Document Template (*.dot).

**6.** In the File **N**ame box, type a name for the template that describes its use (such as *QTRRPT* for a Quarterly Report template, or *RAISE* for a raise request memo to the boss).

**7.** Click OK or press Enter to save your template.

## Using the Template

To base a document on the template you have created, open the **File** menu and choose **New**. In the **New** dialog, choose your template from the list box and click OK. All the styles for this type of document are now available for your use.

## Making Changes to the Template

Need to make changes to your template? It's simple. Open the **File** menu and choose **Open**. In the List Files of **T**ype list box, select Document Template. Double-click your template's name in the file list to open the template. Make changes to the template as you would any Word document—you can add text, create new styles, and redefine existing styles. When you're finished, just click the Save tool to save the altered template.

# PART V

# Help!

**Includes:**

# CHAPTER 17
# Getting Help

## IN A NUTSHELL

▼ Get help
▼ Use the Help Index
▼ Search for help on a topic

nn Landers says it all the time: Don't be embarrassed about getting help. Most Word for Windows users occasionally click open the Help menu, which has a lot of information in it. Spending some time getting familiar with Help can pay off handsomely for you and even for your coworkers, because you'll know how to answer your own questions when they come up—instead of bugging that poor Word user down the hall (who has been heroically patient with you). This chapter runs through the basics of using Help efficiently.

# Quick Ways to Get Help

You can access help about something specific, such as a dialog box or menu option, or you can open the Help Index and find the topic yourself.

---

**Checklist**

▼ When you see a dialog box, information box, question box, or alert box and you're not sure quite what to do, ask for Help. If there's a Help button, you can just click it. If not, press F1. This starts Word Help, and you see a help window.

▼ Wondering what a menu option does? Here's how to find out. Press Shift+F1, which turns the pointer into a big question mark. Then choose the command, just as you would if you were actually using it. Instead of doing the command, Word displays the Help page that explains what the command does.

▼ You can also press Shift+F1 and click a tool on the Toolbar, a button on the Ribbon, or an area of the screen to see what it does.

▼ Shift+F1 doesn't work on dimmed commands. To get help on such a command, click open the menu, use the arrow keys to highlight the dimmed option, and press F1.

▼ To close the Help window, just double-click the Control menu box at the upper-left corner of the screen.

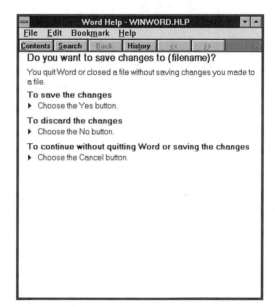

The Help window that appears when you ask for help about a dialog box.

# Using the Help Index

Another more manual way to get Help is to use the Help Index. You can search the index manually or use the Search button to find the topic you need.

To view the Help Index, click open the **Help** menu and choose Help Index. You see the Word Help Index window. Click the topic you want.

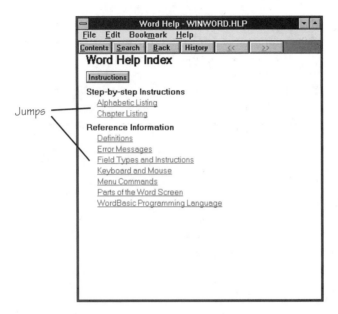

Jumps

**Getting around in Help**

▼ The underlined words you see here and there are *jumps*. When you move the pointer to a jump, it changes into a little hand with an index finger extended upward. If you click the jump, Word jumps to the page relevant to the jump topic.

▼ To go back to the last page you saw, click the **B**ack button.

▼ To go back to a page you saw previously, click the History button and choose the Help page you want to see again.

▼ To see the next Help page, click the Next button (the one with >> on it).

▼ To see the previous Help page, click the Previous button (the one with << on it).

▼ To see the Help Index again, click the Contents button.

## Search Me!

You can search the Help Index manually by jumping from topic to topic until you find the one you want. But you'll probably get lost and never find what you want or your way out. A better bet: Click the Search button. You'll see the Search dialog box.

Type the search word here —

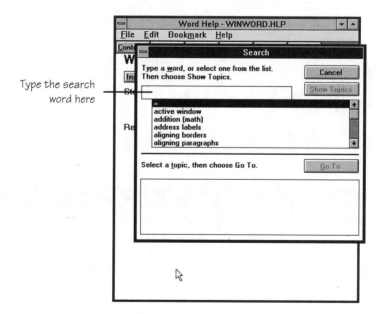

To use the Search dialog box, just type a word in the text box. As you type, Word scrolls the list to the nearest spelling of a topic name and highlights this name. If the name looks promising, click Show Topics to see a list of topics at the bottom of the screen. Select one of these topics, then click Go To to display the screen you want.

**"I HATE THIS!"**

### I can't find the topic I want!

The topics listed in the Search dialog box aren't cross-referenced; there's an *underlining* entry but no *character styles: underlining* entry. If at first you don't find a topic, try to think of other words that describe it, and search for those. If this doesn't work, I've found that Search responds wonderfully when threatened with a large-caliber automatic weapon.

## More Helpful Help on Help

Here's a Help miscellany for your diversion and enlightenment.

**Checklist**

▼ Want an explanation of the parts of Word's screen? From the Help Index, click Parts of the Word Screen.

▼ Want help with keyboard commands? Click Keyboard and Mouse, then click the Keyboard subject you want.

▼ Find something really useful in Help and want to be able to display it again quickly without clicking dozens of times? Display the page,

then click open the Bookmark menu and choose **Define**. When the dialog box appears, just click OK to add this page title to the Bookmark menu. You can then choose this page from this menu quickly, whenever you access Help.

▼ Want to make your own notes in Help? Click open the **Edit** menu and choose **Annotation**. In the Annotate dialog box, type a note of whatever length you like. Click **S**ave to save the annotation. After you do so, you see a little paper clip next to the Help page name; if you click this paper clip, you see your annotation.

▼ Want to print a Help topic? Click open the **File** menu and choose **Print Topic**.

---

### Top Ten Word-Related Problems Not Addressed in Word Help

**10.** Overwhelming urge to immerse entire computer system in solution of caustic soda

**9.** Fear that use of the computer for writing leads to superficial, bloated prose. Hey, it can't be *you* that writes that poorly

**8.** Hypnosis apparently induced by blinking insertion point; coworkers insist that, during hypnotic episodes, you relate tales of previous lives, UFO abduction

**7.** Nagging fear that prolonged use of computer will lead to loss of hair

**6.** Craving to try to get hands on those little paragraph mark buggers and strangle them

**5.** Vexing suspicion that Word could have been designed to be easier to use

*continues*

**Top Ten Mostly Word Problems Not Addressed in Word Help, continued**

**4.** Odd but recurrent nightmare that you have become the mouse pointer and cannot escape being jerked around on the screen

**3.** Tendency to criticize font choices and page layout in every publication you read instead of discussing content, meaning of articles

**2.** Terrifying discovery that pictures on Toolbar are actually an Egyptian hieroglyphic that says something about a "thousand-year curse"

**1.** Devilish but somehow intensely pleasurable fantasies of driving a Jeep Cherokee repeatedly over original program disks, Word manual

# CHAPTER 18

# Fear and Loathing in the Document Window

## IN A NUTSHELL

- ▼ Diagnose and solve common Word problems
- ▼ Know when to throw in the towel

W ord is a big, complex program with its own, unique way of doing things. And frankly, it takes some getting used to. This chapter surveys the cries of rage and horror that are likely to emanate from rooms in which people learn Word. You'll discover the cause of these Word outrages, all of which are actually pretty easy to solve. Before long, you will tame Word (or perhaps Word will tame you), and you will use the program meekly with only an occasional fit of anger.

# It won't let me delete with the Backspace key!

You're wiping out a lot of text by holding down the Backspace key, but you hit a wall—Word beeps and refuses to delete any more! What is wrong? Has Word crashed?

**Cause:** You tried to backspace up into a paragraph that has a different format. Because backspacing would delete the paragraph mark and the paragraph's formats along with the mark, the program is trying to stop you from doing something you might regret.

**Solution:** If you want to keep deleting, press the left-arrow key to move the insertion point into the next paragraph up, then bear down on that Backspace key again.

# I'm trying to insert text, but it's wiping out existing text!

As you type, your letters replace the ones already on the screen.

**Cause:** You accidentally pressed the Ins key, which toggles Word into Overtype mode (look for the OVR code on the status bar).

**Solution:** Press Ins to put Word back into the Insert mode. The OVR code disappears.

# My text runs off the screen!

This is a huge hassle because Word scrolls right as you reach the end of the line, and then scrolls left when you start a new line. You're beginning to get seasick.

**Cause:** You've chosen a teensy-weensy font size, or you've chosen Landscape page orientation (sideways printing). At 100 percent magnification, the lines are longer than Word's window.

 **Solution:** Click the Zoom Page Width tool. This tool automatically sets the page width to accommodate the longest line.

# What happened to my paragraph format?

You're editing away, and bang! The paragraph you're working on suddenly loses its paragraph formats, such as indents, alignment, and line spacing.

**Cause:** You accidentally deleted one of those awful paragraph mark thingies. These not only keep paragraphs separate, but they also "store" paragraph formats. If you delete the mark, you delete the formats, too, and the paragraph takes on the formats of the paragraph below the mark.

**Solution:** Open the **E**dit menu and choose **U**ndo immediately. Word restores the deletion and, along with it, the formats you wiped out. Or, you can copy and paste the paragraph mark from the formatted paragraph above.

**TIP**

While you're editing, display the paragraph marks (by clicking the ¶ button in the Ribbon) so that you can see what you're doing. You're less likely to delete a paragraph mark accidentally if you can see the little blighters on-screen.

# Where's the insertion point?

You can't find it anywhere.

**Cause:** You scrolled using the scroll bars. The insertion point is buried back in your document somewhere.

**Solution:** Just press the right-arrow key. This causes the screen to jump back to where the action is.

# It's clipping off the top of lines that have big font sizes!

This looks really ugly. It's like looking at the members of a play's cast with the curtain half-drawn; you see the feet and lower legs, but that's it.

**Cause:** You decided to get fancy with line spacing and chose the Exactly option in the Line Spacing box (Paragraph dialog box).

**Solution:** Open the Format menu and choose Paragraph. In the Line Spacing box, choose Auto. Click OK or press Enter to confirm your choice.

# I hear all this talk about the Ribbon and the Ruler but I don't see these things!

You hunt for buttons and tools, but they are not there.

**Cause:** You or someone else has turned off these features. A good reason for doing so, at least temporarily, is to increase the amount of space available for your document.

**Solution:** Open the View menu and, if necessary, activate Toolbar, Ribbon, and Ruler. (A menu option in this area is currently active if there's a check mark next to it. If there's no check mark, choosing the option turns it on.)

# My document looks weird and there's a new row of funny buttons!

Even worse, each line has a horrid-looking little box in front of it.

**Cause:** You accidentally switched to Outline view. In the Outline view of your document, you can collapse your document's body text, make an outline of its subject matter, and reorganize your document just by

rearranging headings in the outline. This is pretty cool, but very few Word users actually use it. It's mentioned in the *Quick and Dirty Dozens* section at the end of this book.

**Solution:** Open the **V**iew menu and choose **N**ormal or **P**age Layout.

# My font and font size choices are gone and boldface looks like underlining!

All the text is in one, stupendously ugly font in one size—12 points.

**Cause:** You accidentally switched to **D**raft view, which is used when fast screen performance is the main thing in life.

**Solution:** Open the **V**iew menu and choose **N**ormal or **P**age Layout.

# This stupid printout doesn't have page numbers!

The text looks great, but…

**Cause:** Word doesn't print page numbers automatically—you have to turn on page numbers for each document you create.

**Solution:** If you don't plan to add headers or footers to your document, you can add page numbers quickly using the Page N**u**mbers option in the Insert menu. For more information, flip to Chapter 3. If you're adding headers and footers, you can include page numbers in them, as explained in Chapter 11.

# This font size looks awful!

Your text has a bad case of "the jaggies"—lines that are supposed to look gently curved look like stair-steps instead.

**Cause:** You're using a printer font that doesn't have a screen font backup.

**Solution:** Try printing; the font might look fine when printed, even if it looks horrible on-screen. To avoid the jaggies, use TrueType or Adobe Type Manager (ATM) fonts, which look good on-screen regardless of what font size you choose.

# It printed only a half page and then went on to the next one!

This is called a *bad page break*.

**Cause:** There are a number of possibilities. You may have formatted a paragraph with the **P**age Break Before, Keep With **N**ext, or **K**eep Lines Together options. Or, you may have entered a manual page break that lost its rationale after you inserted or deleted text above the break.

**Solution:** Delete the manual page break, if any. If there's no manual page break, select the paragraphs before and after the break, choose **P**aragraph from the Forma**t** menu, and clear the options in the Pagination area.

# I want to do that neat drag-and-drop editing, but nothing happens!

Dragging the selection does not produce the dramatic results promised in this text.

**Cause:** You or someone else turned off the **D**rag-and-drop Text Editing check box in the Options window.

**Solution:** To turn on this option, open the **T**ools menu and choose **O**ptions. In the **C**ategory list, click the General icon. In the Settings area, activate the **D**rag-and-drop Text Editing option by clicking its box. Then click OK or press Enter.

# The power went off and I lost my work!

This is a baddie. People have been known to do savage things in this situation, such as stomping innocent mice to death.

**Cause:** While you work, your text is kept only in Word's memory, which loses all the information stored in it if the power is cut off.

**Solution:** To prevent work losses due to power outages, open the **T**ools menu and choose **O**ptions. In the **C**ategory list, click the Save icon. In the Set Save options area, click Automatic **S**ave, and use the spinners to choose an interval, such as five minutes. Then click OK or press Enter. Word saves your work automatically every five minutes. What's more, if the power cuts off, you will see your document on-screen the next time you start Word, even if you never chose **S**ave from the **F**ile menu.

I HATE WORD FOR WINDOWS!

**TIP**

Turn on Automatic Save now. Sooner or later, you'll be really glad you did.

## Top Ten Destructive Acts Committed after File Loss (followed by estimated average repair costs)

**10.** Revolver emptied into computer screen ($409, not including $175 fine and 30 days for possession of unregistered firearm)

**9.** Computer connected to high-voltage circuit to "zap its brains out" ($1,487, not including loss of building due to fire)

**8.** Computer system unit struck repeatedly with baseball bat ($1,219, plus $16 for a new bat)

**7.** Computer system unit thrown through plate glass window ($2,676)

**6.** Person who told you to buy Word thrown through plate glass window ($2.8 million, assuming out-of-court settlement)

**5.** Foreign object thrust into floppy disk drive (dry object, $95; food or other moist objects, $387; explosives, $1653)

**4.** Computer's chips immersed in Drano to "teach them a lesson" ($211, not including charge for emergency room care)

**3.** Fist through monitor ($13,421, including average medical care and disability)

**2.** Disk torn to pieces with bare hands and teeth ($0.62 per disk)

**1.** Mouse thrown to ground and stomped to death ($72)

# I tried to use Spelling (or Graph, or Draw, or Thesaurus), but it's not installed!

A real drag. You're all excited about using these things, and then Wham! Total frustration.

**Cause:** When Word for Windows was installed, these features weren't installed along with the program, which was dumb.

**Solution:** Quit Word. In the Word Program Group, double-click the Word Setup icon. You'll see the Microsoft Word Setup window. Click Continue until Setup starts checking for available disk space. When you see the dialog box with three big buttons labeled Complete Installation, Custom Installation, and Minimum Installation, click Custom Installation. Click the options you want to install, and click Setup to add these options to your Word installation. You'll be prompted to insert the original Word program disks, so have these handy.

**"I HATE THIS!"**

### It says there isn't enough disk space for this stuff!

Ah, that's probably why they're not available. Well, you have several options. You can delete unused files from your hard drive, or you can get a bigger hard drive.

# When to Bring in Your Local Word Wizard

This is pretty easy to decide. If you keep hitting a wall as you attempt to solve the problem, stop. Don't distress yourself unduly by spending hours trying to do something repeatedly without success. The problem lies in

something you don't know about or don't understand, and all you're doing is creating bad feelings toward the computer that will someday lead you to throw the whole system out a plate glass window, causing psychological stress to your neighbors and leading to endless lawsuits. Get up, get away from the computer, and get your local Word wizard to sit down with you and show you how to fix the problem.

# CHAPTER 19

# Where's My File?

## IN A NUTSHELL

▼ Understand why files get lost

▼ Take a look at Find File

▼ Search your whole hard disk

▼ Search for a file that contains text you specify

▼ Know when to get an expert's help

I HATE WORD FOR WINDOWS!

The call, invariably, comes at about 2:30 a.m. "Bryan," says the harried voice. "My file. It's gone. I'm really sorry to be calling you so late. But there's no one else who can help me. Please?"

This chapter is for all my friends who turn to me in their hour of need. Would you at least try reading this before calling me? In this chapter, you'll find out exactly what I would do if I arrived bleary-eyed at your house at 4 a.m. and tried, heroically, to help you recover your file. Thanks.

# Why Files Get Lost

Probably, you weren't paying attention when you saved the file. You saved it to a directory other than the directory where you usually save files.

There are other possibilities, too, which we'll explore one by one. You might have given the file a name other than the one you think you assigned it. You may have given the file an extension other than Word's default extension, .DOC. If you're really brilliant at self-destruction, you may have failed to save the file at all—but that's not likely.

**TIP**

If you're in the grip of deep file loss panic, cheer up. The worst-case scenario isn't the most likely outcome. Chances are pretty good that you'll find your file. Word has some pretty cool file-finding capabilities.

# Introducing the Amazing Find File Command

Let me introduce my friend, Find File. This is a Word command, tucked away in the File menu, that is capable of amazing feats. It can search your entire hard disk, minutely examining every word in every file, to help you retrieve that lost file. With Find File, you can rest assured: If it's on your disk, you can find it.

To start Find File, click open the **F**ile menu and choose **F**ind File. You see the rather massive Find File dialog box.

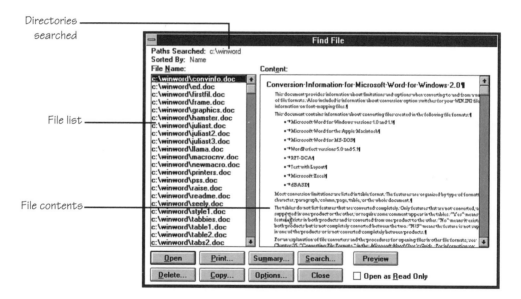

Directories searched

File list

File contents

**A quick guide to the mysteries of the Find File dialog box**

▼    At the top of the dialog box, Word indicates the parts of the disk that it searched in compiling the file list (under File **N**ame). By default, Word searches only Word's directory (c:\winword).

*continues*

I HATE WORD FOR WINDOWS!

**A quick guide to the mysteries of the Find File dialog box, continued**

▼ In the Content box, you see the actual text of the currently selected document in the File **N**ame box. If you click other file names in the File **N**ame list, you see the contents in the Content box. Using the scroll bar, you can actually scroll through the text of the document without opening it. Admittedly, the text is almost too teensy-weensy to read.

▼ To view the Summary Info for the currently selected file, click Summary. You'll see the Summary Info dialog box for this file. This is the dialog box that you fill out when you save the file for the first time.

▼ There are lots of buttons at the bottom of the Find File dialog box, as you've probably noticed. Some of these buttons are cool for managing files (namely **D**elete and **C**opy), whereas **O**pen does the same thing that the File menu's Open command does. You can print a file from this dialog box by selecting it and clicking **P**rint. But all this is beside the point of finding the lost file, which is the subject of this chapter and the focus of your concerns.

▼ Getting out of Find File is by no means obvious, because you might conclude that the Close button is the opposite of **O**pen, and has to do with closing files. Nay, it closes this dialog box, and that's where you should click if you want out, fast. But stick around! We need to find your file, right?

# Broadening the Search (Cast your net wide)

You're hunting for a lost file—a seriously lost file. Much is at risk. Your boss is going to murder you if that report is not on her desk tomorrow morning. So let's get to work.

In this section, you learn how to search your whole darned hard disk for anything, and I mean anything, that resembles a Word document.

To search your entire hard disk for Word documents, follow these steps:

**1.** In the Find File dialog box, click Search. You see the Search dialog box.

To search your entire disk, choose All Drives here

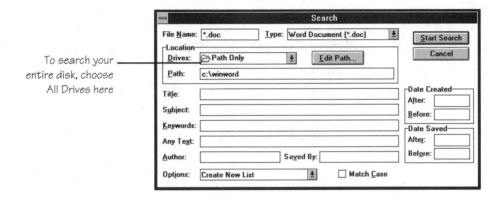

**2.** In the Drives list box, do one of the following:

▼ If your computer is connected to a network, choose All Drives.

▼ If your computer isn't connected to a network, choose All Local Drives.

▼ If you're not sure, what the heck, choose All Drives.

**3.** Click Start Search. Word displays the Building Search Path dialog box, and the program labors mightily to build a list of every .DOC file on your hard disk. When the list is complete, you see the Find File dialog box again. The list now includes every .DOC file on your hard disk.

**4.** Scroll through the File **N**ame list to see if you can find your file. Select any likely candidates and view the contents in the Content list box.

**"I HATE THIS!"**

### There are too many files! I can't make any sense out of this list!

If you're having trouble wading through the list of files in the File **N**ame list, try changing the sort order. By default, Word organizes these files by file name. However, you can organize the file list in other ways, too. For example, you can list them by size, by the last saved date, by author, or by creation date. All these options list the files in descending order (largest file first, or most recently saved file first). To choose one of these options, click the Options button and choose an option in the Options dialog box. Click OK to confirm your choice and return to the Find File dialog box, where the reorganized file list reflects your preference.

## Still Can't Find Your File? (Don't give up yet)

If the previous techniques haven't helped you to find your file, there's still hope. Perhaps you saved the file with a name very different from the one you're thinking you used. Perhaps you just haven't noticed the file in the lengthy file list. In either case, it's time to trot out the big gun: searching every file for text within the document.

To use this effectively, you must first think of one or two words that you used only in the document you're looking for, and in no other documents (or just one or two other documents). Suppose, for instance, you

are looking for the letter you wrote to Sheldon Smith regarding that small matter of that book he borrowed but never returned. To the best of your knowledge, you mentioned that book (*Stalking the Wild Asparagus*) in this document, but no other. *Stalking the Wild Asparagus*, then, is a great search phrase.

To search your entire hard disk for a file that contains text you specify, follow these steps:

**1.** In the Find File dialog box, click **S**earch. You see the Search dialog box.

**2.** In the Drives list box, do one of the following:

▼ If your computer is connected to a network, choose All Drives.

▼ If your computer isn't connected to a network, choose All Local Drives.

**3.** In the Any Text box, carefully type the text you want to match. You don't have to use the same capitalization pattern, but you must type the text exactly as it is spelled in the target document. For example, if you're hunting for documents that mention the Rodent Rights League, you must type those three words exactly, and not *Rodents Right League*.

**4.** When you've double-checked the search text and you're sure it's correct, click the Start Search dialog box. Word starts searching. This is going to take time, because Word has to search every file word-for-word. As the search proceeds, the Building File List dialog box tells you how many files Word has retrieved. When the search is complete, you see the Find File dialog box, which displays a list of the files, if any, that contain the text you specified.

**"I HATE THIS!"**

### I still don't see my file!

Oh, dear. Are you sure you typed the search text right? Do me a favor, OK? Would you try this search again with different search text—text that you're sure is in the document you're looking for? And check your typing in the Any Text box very, very carefully. The least little misspelling or typo will result in zero documents retrieved.

# The Last-Ditch, Whole-Disk Search

If you're reading this, your file has eluded some pretty powerful searches. But don't give up hope—there's still one possibility left. You might have saved your file with an extension other than Word's default extension, .DOC. This could happen, for example, if you got overly creative with file names and thought it would be cute to name a document something like MEOW.CAT. It could also happen if you accidentally or unthinkingly typed a period after the file name, like MEOW. This would prevent Word from assigning the default .DOC extension, and you wouldn't see the file in any of the file lists you've constructed thus far.

Why haven't we tried this search previously? Because it takes a long time. You're asking Word to search all the text of all the files on your entire hard disk for one or two little words that you specified. Obviously, this is going to take time—as much as several minutes—so that's why I don't recommend it unless you're unable to find the file any other way.

To search every file on your entire hard disk for a file that contains text you specify, follow these steps:

**1.** In the Find File dialog box, click **S**earch. You see the Search dialog box.

**2.** In the **D**rives list box, do one of the following:

▼ If your computer is connected to a network, choose All Drives.

▼ If your computer isn't connected to a network, choose All Local Drives.

**3.** In the Any **T**ext box, carefully type the text you want to match.

**4.** In the **T**ype list box, choose All Files (*.*).

**5.** Click **S**tart Search.

**"I HATE THIS!"**

### This didn't work either!

I'm sorry, but I think you either failed to save your file or you deleted it accidentally. If you have DOS 6 (a good idea, incidentally), switch to Program Manager and run Microsoft Windows Undelete (MWUNDEL) immediately. If you don't have DOS 6, or if you don't have any other file undeletion program, don't do anything else to your computer—don't start any other programs or even turn it off. Just go get help immediately from someone who knows how to recover deleted files. Good luck!

**TIP**

To avoid losing any work, you should set up a regular backup program in which you copy new or altered files to floppy disks. Just remember, floppy disks are cheap, but your time isn't.

I HATE WORD FOR WINDOWS!

## Top Ten Rationalizations after Loss of Important File

**10.** Think of all the trees I'm saving by not having to print this out again

**9.** The Pulitzer Prize committee has already met this year

**8.** I didn't really want to share my insights with anyone, anyway

**7.** Although my novel idea is great, everyone knows you can't get published unless you're related by blood to someone at the publishing house

**6.** It's a sign from my Higher Power

**5.** It would have needed another draft, and I'm sick of it

**4.** Sure, sure, sure. I spent umpteen hours getting the words just right. But it's probably best I start from scratch. Yeah, a clean break will be good for me. Yeah, a clean break…

**3.** I needed a good cry, anyway

**2.** Even if I had completed it, someone else would have gotten the recognition

**1.** That type of work is so far ahead of its time that it would have been appreciated only after my death

# PART VI

# Quick and Dirty Dozens

## Includes:

Cool Things That Word Can Do

Hottest Mouse Shortcuts

Features You Shouldn't Monkey with unless You Have Time to Kill

Least Popular Word Messages (and what to do)

Things You Really Shouldn't Do

Really Useful Keyboard Tricks

## I HATE
## WORD FOR WINDOWS

# Quick and Dirty
# Dozens

## IN A NUTSHELL

▼ 12 More Cool Things That Word
Can Do

▼ 12 Hottest Mouse Shortcuts

▼ 12 Features You Shouldn't
Monkey with Unless You
Have Time to Kill

▼ 12 Least Popular Word
Messages (and what to do)

▼ 12 Things You Really
Shouldn't Do

▼ 12 Really Useful Keyboard
Tricks

# 12 More Cool Things That Word Can Do

**1.** Add the date and time.

Don't type the date or time when Word can insert it for you automatically. Open the Insert menu, click Date and **T**ime, and choose a date or time format from the **A**vailable Formats list box. Click OK or press Enter to add the date or time to your document. The date changes to the current date each time you print the document.

**2.** Add a footnote.

Word is a great program for anyone who has to document work with footnotes (at the bottom of the page) or endnotes (at the end of the section or the document). Word automatically numbers the footnotes with a superscripted footnote reference mark. To create a footnote, place the insertion point where you want the reference mark to appear, open the Insert menu, and choose **Footnote**. In the Footnote dialog box, just click OK or press Enter to confirm creating a footnote with automatic numbering. Word then opens the Footnotes window, enabling you to type the text of the note. Click Close to return to your document.

To edit the footnote, just select the footnote reference mark and double-click. Word opens the Footnote window and displays the note. To delete the footnote entirely, select the reference mark (not the footnote) and press Del.

**3.** Print the footnotes at the end of a section or the end of the document.

By default, Word places footnotes at the bottom of the page. You can also print the footnotes beneath the text (if the text doesn't take up the whole page, which is often the case at the end of a

chapter), at the end of a section, or at the end of the document. To control where footnotes print, open the Insert menu, click Footnote, and click the Options button in the Footnote dialog box. In the Footnote Options dialog box, choose a location in the Place At list. Click OK until you see your document again.

**4.** **Use Find File to make a quick, simple backup copy of an important document.**

I can't emphasize enough the importance of backing up your work. It's not enough just to make another copy on your hard disk. What if your hard disk fails? What if you accidentally erase the file? (It happens all the time, believe me.)

Do yourself a favor: Go get a couple of boxes of preformatted disks that match your computer's disk drives (for example, if you have a high-density 3.5-inch drive, get high-density, 3.5-inch disks). They're really not that expensive when you think what it would cost you in time and energy to retype a lost file!

After you save an important document, do this: Open the File menu and choose Find File. Use the File Name list box to locate and select your file. (For information about locating files with Find File, see Chapter 19.) Click Copy, and put a disk in your floppy disk drive. In the Drives list, choose the disk drive where you inserted the floppy, and click OK. Word copies your file to the floppy disk. Label and date the disk clearly, and put it where spilled coffee can't get to it.

**5.** **Make a bookmark.**

A bookmark is a unit of text that you have selected and named. After naming a bookmark, you can jump to the bookmark quickly just by choosing its name in the Go To dialog box (to display this dialog box, open the Edit menu and choose Go To, or just press

F5). You can also cross-reference ("See the discussion of such-and-such on page 17") the bookmark text; Word fills in the correct page number for the cross reference automatically.

To create the bookmark, select the text. This can be just a word or a paragraph or more. Then open the **Insert** menu, choose Book-mark, and type a bookmark name (of up to 20 characters) in the Bookmark Name box. Click OK to confirm the bookmark name.

**6.** **Add a cross-reference to bookmark text.**

To create a cross-reference to the bookmark text, place the insertion point where you want the cross-reference page number to appear (as in "See page __"). Press Ctrl+F9. Inside the field character brackets, type `pageref` followed by a space and the bookmark name. A correct cross-reference looks like this: `See page {pageref vacationpolicy}`.

**7.** **Record a macro.**

A macro is a recorded series of mouse movements or keystrokes, which you can save, name, and play back when you want. You can use a macro to automate a command procedure you frequently use. For example, suppose you want to print a draft of your document complete with summary info. However, it's a hassle to do this because you must switch to the Options dialog box before printing the draft, choose the options you want, and then switch back to turn these options off after printing. This is a perfect job for a Print Draft macro.

To record a macro, open the **T**ools menu, click **R**ecord Macro, and type a macro name in the Record Macro **N**ame text box. If you want to assign a key to the macro, choose a key in the Key list box. Then click OK. Now just choose the options you want, as you would normally. Word performs the actions you request. When you are finished, open the **T**ools menu and choose Stop **R**ecorder.

**8.** Use a macro you've recorded.

To "play back" your macro, just press the keyboard shortcut to which you assigned the macro (this will use the Ctrl+Shift keys), or open the Tools menu, choose **M**acro, and highlight the macro name in the Macro **N**ame list. Then click **R**un or press Enter.

If the macro doesn't run as you anticipated, just record it again using the same name, but correct your errors; Word will prompt you to confirm overwriting the old version.

**9.** Assign your styles to a key.

If you like choosing things with keyboard shortcuts, you'll like this: You can assign your styles to keys. To assign a style to a key, open the Format menu, choose Style, and choose a style name in the Style Name list box. Then choose a key in the **K**ey list box, and click **D**efine. When the rest of the dialog box appears, click Change followed by Close.

**10.** Collect text or graphics from here and there and insert them *en masse.*

If you ever want to cut text or graphics from several different locations in one document—or several different documents—and then insert them elsewhere, remember this somewhat weird Word capability: the Spike. This would be great if, say, you decided that the various sections where you raised a topic could be collected and put into their own chapter. The Spike is a special glossary entry that enables you to do this.

To use the Spike, select the first text passage or graphic that you want to collect, and press Ctrl+F3. Word cuts the selection to the Spike. Repeat this as many times as you want in this or other documents. Remember that Word stores all this stuff in the order you collect it.

To insert all the text and graphics that you have collected in the Spike, place the insertion point where you want this stuff to appear. Press Ctrl+Shift+F3. Word places the Spike's contents at this location and clears the Spike.

**11.** **Add an annotation.**

Much writing is done collaboratively these days, and chances are you're going to give your document to someone for comments. Instead of scribbling comments on paper, Word users can actually put them into a Word document, in the form of annotations. Annotations don't print unless you want them to, and you can get rid of them after you've read them.

To create an annotation, open the Insert menu and choose Annotation. Word opens the Annotation pane and enters a reference mark in the text as well as the annotation pane. This contains your initials as well as a reference number. In the Annotation pane, type your annotation text. Then click **C**lose to return to the document.

If you've just gotten a document back from somebody who reviewed it and put in annotations, here's how to read them. From the **V**iew menu, choose **A**nnotations. Word opens the Annotation pane and displays the annotation marks. To read an annotation, select the mark and read the text in the Annotation window.

To get rid of an annotation, just select the mark and press Del.

**12.** **Get a word count.**

"5,000 words max," your editor says. Are you over? Find out fast this way. Save your document. Then open the **F**ile menu, click Summary Info, then click Statistics. You'll see the Document Statistics dialog box, which lists lots of information about your document, including (depressingly) the total editing time (in minutes), the number of revisions, and the last saved date. At the bottom of

the screen, you see the page, word, and character count as of the last save. If any of this stuff is dimmed, click **Update**. To exit, click OK until you see your document again.

# 12 Hottest Mouse Shortcuts

**1.** **Open the Paragraph dialog box.**

Double-click anywhere on the upper half of the Ruler.

**2.** **Open the Go To dialog box.**

Double-click the page number on the status bar.

**3.** **Open the Character dialog box.**

Double-click on the Ribbon background (but not on a button or box)

**4.** **Split the current window into two panes.**

Double-click the split bar at the top of the vertical scroll bar.

**5.** **Maximize or restore a window.**

Double-click the title bar.

**6.** **Open the Symbol dialog box.**

Double-click a symbol that you have inserted into the document.

**7.** **Display footnote text.**

Double-click the footnote reference mark.

**8.** Display annotation text.

Double-click the annotation reference mark.

**9.** Select a word.

Double-click the word.

**10.** Select a sentence.

Hold down the Ctrl key and click anywhere within the sentence.

**11.** Select a paragraph.

Move the pointer to the selection bar next to the paragraph, then double-click.

**12.** Start Microsoft Draw or Microsoft Graph and edit a picture you inserted.

Double-click the picture.

# 12 Features You Shouldn't Monkey with Unless You Have Time to Kill

**TIP**

This section isn't really designed to tell you how to do this stuff, which can get pretty complicated. These features are things you might want to explore if they seem useful to you.

**1.** **Outlines.**

In Word's Outline view, which you can choose from the **V**iew menu, you can create and edit an outline view of your document. In Outline view, titles, headings, and subheadings appear as headings in an outline, which you can indent as you please to show the logical relationships among sections. You can "collapse" body text, so that only the headings appear.

An outline is really just a different way of looking at your document, which is pretty neat for the following reason: If you make changes to your document, the changes are reflected in the outline—and vice versa. But this takes some getting used to. And, it works well only if you've used Word's built-in Heading styles to type your title (Heading 1), major headings (Heading 2), and subheadings (Heading 3).

This feature is well worth exploring if you write documents such as proposals, scientific articles, business reports, or theses, which have lots of internal subheadings.

**2.** **Mail merging.**

This is a classic office application for cranking out form letters, in which the same text is sent to every recipient but every letter looks as though it were individually typed, with the correspondent's name and address typed neatly. To pull this off, you have to create a data file according to strict rules, and then you create a main document that contains the text you're going to send to everyone. This document also contains merge fields, which tell Word what kind of information to insert (such as *Last Name* or *Address*).

**3.** Indexes.

Word can compile an index from words or phrases you have marked in your text. To mark the text, you use a command that surrounds the text with hidden text and a special code. When you're finished, you use another command that compiles the index, complete with accurate page numbers. If you later change the text in a way that affects pagination, you must recompile the index.

This is really useful if you prepare in-house publications that require indexes, such as training manuals or company benefits booklets.

**4.** Tables of contents.

This feature works like indexes: You use a command that marks the table of contents entries, and then you use another command that compiles the table of contents (complete with accurate page numbers). If you created your document using the built-in heading styles, as mentioned in the discussion of Outlines, this is even easier because Word can compile the table of contents from the outline. As with the index, if you later change the text in a way that affects pagination, you must recompile the table of contents.

This is really useful if you're creating documents for internal use, such as employee applications, office memos, or employee reviews.

**5.** Forms.

You can combine some of Word's features, such as tables, borders, and shading, to desktop-publish your own forms. You can then print them. There's also a way you can set a form up so that it's easy to fill out on-screen, with the insertion point advancing automatically to the next data entry area.

**6.** **Revision marks.**

If you're reviewing someone else's work, you can turn on revision marks. Anything you delete won't actually be deleted; it is just shown with strikethrough formatting. Anything you add appears with special formatting. Later, the person who wrote the document can review the marks, selectively incorporating your changes or discarding them.

**7.** **Mailing labels.**

Word can print on all kinds of commercial mailing labels. To get this to work, though, you have to set up a print merge application (see "Mail merging" in item 2), which is a hassle. Even worse, Word doesn't provide good tools for massaging your mailing list data.

Don't torment yourself trying to print mailing labels with Word. There are special-purpose applications, and even special-purpose printers, that make this job much easier.

**8.** **Linking.**

This is a neat Windows 3.1 capability that sounds much more complicated than it is. Basically, it comes into play when you copy something such as an Excel or Lotus 1-2-3 spreadsheet into your Word document. If you paste this with linking turned on, you create a *hot link* between the original spreadsheet and the copy that's in your Word document. (No, a hot link isn't one of those great Bratwursts you can get at Coney Island.) When you make a change to the original spreadsheet, Windows automatically updates the copy in your Word document, so the copy always reflects the up-to-the-minute figures.

**9.** **Embedding.**

Embedding is like linking, but with one difference: The other application's file is actually placed into your Word document. If this sounds weird and incomprehensible, relax, because you've already done it without realizing that you were "embedding." In Chapter 15, you created Microsoft Drawing and Microsoft Graph pictures from within Word, with the result that the picture became part of your Word document. To edit the picture, and use all the tools of the external application, you merely double-click the embedded picture.

You can embed other things, such as spreadsheets. Imagine having a whole spreadsheet embedded in your Word document, so that just by double-clicking it you can use all the tools of Excel, Quattro Pro, or whatever. Cool.

**10.** **Customizing menus.**

Word comes with dozens of commands, not all of which are on the menus. If you like, you can customize the menus, deleting commands you're not using and adding others that you like. You do this using the Menus part of the Options dialog box (Tools menu).

I don't recommend this, because your copy of Word will become weird and idiosyncratic. If you have to use Word on someone else's computer, you'll experience some disorientation because the menus will probably be the default menus.

**11.** **Customizing keyboard shortcuts.**

This is the same deal as the menus—you can customize Word's keyboard layout to your heart's content. You do this with the Keyboard part of the Options dialog box.

I don't recommend this for the same reason I don't recommend customizing the menus—you'll experience disorientation if you use a different copy of Word. But it's certainly OK to create keyboard shortcuts for your styles and macros.

**12.** **Writing macros.**

Word comes with a huge programming language called WordBasic, which is all you need if you really want to torment yourself into computer imbecility. The script runs like this: You stop seeing your friends, you stop wanting to do anything else besides play with writing WordBasic macros. Pretty soon, you forget the practical reason you started doing this, and just lose yourself playing with arrays, variables, and stuff like that. Finally, you stop taking care of yourself, and former friends shake their heads in dismay.

WordBasic can do amazing things, as you can tell by opening one of the letter templates. Dialog boxes pop up and wonderful things happen. Let someone else do this!

# 12 Least Popular Word Messages (and what to do)

**1.** Do you want to save changes?

You tried to escape from Word without saving something. Click Yes to save, **N**o to abandon this document, or Cancel to go back to Word and rethink the whole thing.

**2.** `The printer is offline or not selected.`

You tried to print, but you got this message again. Check your printer. Is it turned on? Is it selected (look for a "select" or "on-line" button and make sure that it's illuminated). Is there paper? If all these are OK, check the cable that connects the printer to the computer. After that, get someone to help you—you'll need it.

**3.** `Do you want to continue checking at the beginning?`

You started a spelling check midway through the document. Word has checked the spelling only from the insertion point's location down. Click **Yes** to resume checking from the beginning of the document, or click **No** to stop checking—but bear in mind that part of your document hasn't been proofed.

**4.** `Do you want to save the global glossary and command changes?`

You don't remember creating a "global glossary," do you? But do click **Yes** here. You created a glossary or macro, and it isn't saved if you don't click the **Yes** button. If you're sure you want to abandon *all* of the glossaries and macros that you created in this session, click **No**.

**5.** `This is not a valid measurement` or `This is not a valid integer.`

In a dialog box that requires you to type a measurement, you typed something that Word can't recognize. Type only numbers and the measurement abbreviations that Word recognizes, such as *li* (lines), *pt* (points), *in* (inches), and *cm* (centimeters).

**6.** `This session is too complex. Please close a window.`

You've used up all your system resources trying to do too many things at once. Save your work and close one or more windows.

**7.** `Low memory.`

Word is running out of memory. Save your work immediately. Try closing one or more windows that you're not using.

**8.** `System Error: Cannot read from Drive ` *`such-and-such.`*

Probably, you removed a floppy disk from a disk drive that you used sometime in this session. This is a no-no. Word expects the disk to still be there, even if you're not using it—which is dumb, but then lots of things about computers are dumb. Put the disk back in the drive and click **Retry**.

**9.** `The search text is not found.`

You tried to search or replace, but Word couldn't find anything to match. In the Find or Replace dialog boxes, carefully check your spelling.

**10.** `This is not a valid action for footnotes.`

You tried to delete a footnote by removing all the text and the trailing paragraph mark. However, this is a no-no. To delete a footnote, delete the footnote reference mark back in your document's text.

**11.** `You have placed a large amount of text into the Clipboard.`

You've just exited Word, and you get this message. Here's why. You cut or copied some stuff to the Clipboard during this session, and

Word is afraid that you might have done this so that you could paste it into some other application after you quit Word. If so, click **Yes**. If this wasn't your intent, click **No**.

**12.** `Word cannot start the Speller (or Grammar checker or Thesaurus).`

Probably, these options weren't installed. For more information, see Chapter 18.

# 12 Things You Really Shouldn't Do

**1.** **Don't edit with paragraph marks turned off.**

It's just too easy to wipe out a paragraph break, leading to loss of formatting. To turn on paragraph marks, click the paragraph mark tool on the Toolbar.

**2.** **Don't press Enter at the end of every line.**

Let Word "wrap" text down to the next line automatically. Press Enter only when you want to start a new paragraph.

**3.** **Don't press Enter to create blank lines.**

Instead, press Ctrl+O (the letter). This enables you to adjust the spacing later, or remove it entirely if you want, without having to delete every blank line. If you want to double-space your lines, press Ctrl+2.

**4.** **Don't indent text with the space bar.**

Word can't align text indented this way. To indent all the lines of the paragraph from the left margin, click the Indent tool on the Toolbar. To indent just the first line, you can press Tab, or drag the first line indent marker on the Ruler.

**5.** **Don't work without saving periodically.**

Your computer might crash, the power might go off, you might accidentally hit the Reset button with the tip of your cane—who knows? And then, bye-bye.

**6.** **Don't break pages manually.**

Sometimes this is OK, such as when you're starting a new chapter. However, it's really best to control page breaks with the Pagination options in the Paragraph dialog box, such as Keep With Next or Keep Lines Together. These insert page breaks only where needed, so they don't result in bad page breaks if you later insert or delete some text above the break.

**7.** **Don't replace without confirmation.**

When you're using the Replace command, resist the temptation to let Word perform the replacements without asking for your confirmation first. It's really hard to predict how a given Replace operation is going to work.

**8.** **Don't wait to use Undo.**

If you've just performed an operation such as a sort, you can't Undo unless you choose **U**ndo immediately. If you type some text or choose another command, it's too late.

**9.** **Don't put off backing up your work.**

What would you do if every one of your files was destroyed? It happens a lot. Sometimes, disks fail. In addition, people have been known to accidentally delete huge portions of their disks while "housecleaning." Begin a regular backup program and carry it out religiously.

**10.** **Don't bother trying to memorize Word's keyboard commands.**

There are better mouse and menu equivalents for all of these. The keyboard commands are included just for competitive reasons, really. Word's keyboard isn't particularly well mapped out or useful. There are a only few commands that you may find worth learning, and I've listed them in a previous Dozen.

**11.** **Don't save documents to Word's directories.**

While "housecleaning," you might delete one of the one zillion or so support files that Word needs to run. Better: Create a new directory for your Word documents, and change Word's properties in Program Manager so that this directory becomes the default directory for file-storage purposes. Get a Windows zombie to help you do this.

**12.** **Don't, don't, DON'T display the secret animation screen.**

This is not something you are supposed to know about. But because you insist, do the following:

**1.** From the Tools menu, choose **R**ecord Macro.

**2.** In the Record Macro **N**ame box, type SPIFF and click OK.

**3.** From the Tools menu, choose Stop **R**ecorder.

4. From the Tools menu, choose **Macro**.

5. From the list, choose SPIFF and click **Edit**.

6. Delete the `Sub Main` and `End Sub` thingies. What's left is what looks like a blank document.

7. From the File menu, choose **Close**.

8. Click **Yes** to save the changes.

9. From the Help menu, choose **About**.

10. In the About dialog box, click the Word icon.

# 12 Really Useful Keyboard Tricks

1. **Grow the font, shrink the font.**

   To increase the font size of the selected text, press Ctrl+F2. To decrease the font size of the selected text, press Shift+Ctrl+F2.

2. **Repeat whatever you just did.**

   Press F4. This is a great way to repeat a format throughout a document, here and there.

3. **Minimize the Word window.**

   Need to do something with another application? Get Word out of the way fast by pressing Alt+F9. To get back to Word, double-click the Word icon that appears at the bottom of the screen in Windows.

**4.** Cancel paragraph formatting.

To cancel all paragraph formats (such as alignments, indents, and line spacing) and restore the Normal style for the selection, press Ctrl+Q.

**5.** Cancel character formatting.

To cancel all character formats, including fonts, font sizes, emphases, position, and spacing for the selection, press Ctrl+space bar.

**6.** Get Help on the next thing you click or choose.

Press Shift+F1. The cursor turns into a question mark. Now click something or choose something from a menu. You'll see a relevant Help page.

**7.** Change the case of the selection.

Press Shift+F3 until you see the case pattern you want.

**8.** Select a column of text.

This is really useful if you want to select a column of numbers in a tabbed table. Press Ctrl+Shift+F8 to turn on the column selection mode, and then use the mouse to select the column.

**9.** Delete the word to the left or the right of the insertion point.

Instead of fussing with the mouse to remove words as you're editing, try these keyboard commands: Ctrl+Backspace deletes the word to the left of the insertion point, whereas Ctrl+Del deletes the word to the right.

**10.** Cut the selection to the Clipboard.

Press Ctrl+X.

**11.** Copy the selection to the Clipboard.

Press Ctrl+C.

**12.** Paste the Clipboard's contents at the insertion point's location.

Press Ctrl+V.

# I HATE

# Index

I HATE WORD FOR WINDOWS!

## G

I HATE WORD FOR WINDOWS!